T0090524

THE NOT SO GOOD,
THE BAD,
AND THE
DOWNRIGHT UGLY

What NOT to Do to Be an Effective Leader

DR. JOEY BEESON

WESTBOW
PRESS®
A DIVISION OF THOMAS NELSON
& ZONDERVAN

Copyright © 2024 Dr. Joey Beeson.

All rights reserved. No part of this book may be used or reproduced by
any means, graphic, electronic, or mechanical, including photocopying,
recording, taping or by any information storage retrieval system
without the written permission of the author except in the case
of brief quotations embodied in critical articles and reviews.

This book is a work of non-fiction. Unless otherwise noted, the author
and the publisher make no explicit guarantees as to the accuracy of
the information contained in this book and in some cases, names
of people and places have been altered to protect their privacy.

WestBow Press books may be ordered through
booksellers or by contacting:

WestBow Press
A Division of Thomas Nelson & Zondervan
1663 Liberty Drive
Bloomington, IN 47403
www.westbowpress.com
844-714-3454

Because of the dynamic nature of the Internet, any web addresses or
links contained in this book may have changed since publication and
may no longer be valid. The views expressed in this work are solely those
of the author and do not necessarily reflect the views of the publisher,
and the publisher hereby disclaims any responsibility for them.

Any people depicted in stock imagery provided by Getty Images are
models, and such images are being used for illustrative purposes only.
Certain stock imagery © Getty Images.

Interior Image Credit: Sebastian Catangay

ISBN: 979-8-3850-1899-4 (sc)
ISBN: 979-8-3850-1900-7 (e)

Library of Congress Control Number: 2024903167

Print information available on the last page.

WestBow Press rev. date: 02/20/2024

Unless otherwise indicated, scripture quotations are from the
ESV Bible® (The Holy Bible, English Standard Version®), copyright
© 2001 by Crossway Bibles, a publishing ministry of Good
News Publishers. Used by permission. All rights reserved.

Scripture quotations marked KJV are taken from
the Holy Bible, King James Version.

Scripture quotations marked NIV are taken from the Holy Bible, New
International Version®, NIV®. Copyright © 1973, 1978, 1984 by Biblica,
Inc.™ Used by permission of Zondervan. All rights reserved worldwide.

Scripture quotations marked NLT are taken from the Holy
Bible, New Living Translation, copyright © 1996, 2004, 2007 by
Tyndale House Foundation. Used by permission of Tyndale House
Publishers, Inc., Carol Stream, Illinois 60188. All rights reserved.

Scripture quotations marked AMP are taken from the
Amplified® Bible, Copyright © 1954, 1958, 1962, 1964, 1965,
1987 by The Lockman Foundation. Used by permission.

Scripture quotations marked NASB are taken from the New American
Standard Bible®, Copyright © 1960, 1962, 1963, 1968, 1971, 1972, 1973,
1975, 1977, 1995 by The Lockman Foundation. Used by permission.

DEDICATION

I dedicate this book to my amazing, talented, beautiful, supportive, and godly wife, Sarah. She is a Proverbs 31 model of strength and leadership.

A special shoutout is also given to my five wonderful children, godly parents, and ever-supportive and dependable in-laws.

CONTENTS

Foreword xi
Acknowledgments xv
Introduction xvii

Chapter 1 How This Book Came to Fruition 1

Chapter 2 Leadership Theories, Presence,
and Influence 16

Chapter 3 Key Leadership
Characteristics and Followership 50

Chapter 4 Biblical Principles of Leadership 79

Chapter 5 Unpacking the Five Bad
Leadership Characters 95

Chapter 6 Examples of Bad Leadership
from History and Scripture 114

Chapter 7 Contemporary Stories
of Bad Leadership 128

Chapter 8 The Master Leader's Example 143

Chapter 9 Final Thoughts, Reflections, and
Questions to Ponder 152

References 163

For the past forty years, I have been involved in multiple leadership roles in the PK-12 systems as an assistant principal and principal. Then, I moved to higher education, where I took on roles of director, department and division chair, and dean, with a focused time as a vice president at the university level. Blessed with leadership skills and aspirations, I strove to follow my north star in pursuing excellence in my professional and personal life. As a Christian man, I was called to Christian education and failed and succeeded in my human frailty, but I humbled myself to serve my Lord the entire time. In my final professional role, I relished the opportunity to collaborate on establishing a rigorous curriculum in doctoral students for leadership implemented with success, all from the gifts of many and the talents of my colleagues, all the while striving to emulate a Christian ideal in my efforts.

I have been associated with Dr. Joey Beeson as a colleague, friend, and journeyman on our faith journey for several years. Dr. Beeson is a beloved instructor, and students sought him out for his insights, integrity, and moral leadership. His colleagues respected his tenacity in his commitment to his students, but more importantly, his infusion of Christ-centered teachings into the curriculum. His selflessness and his willingness to serve are just a few examples of why his text is needed in today's convoluted world. Most importantly, his unfailing dedication to his family and to the Lord positions him as a strong voice for these critical discussions on leadership effectiveness.

In *The Not So Good, The Bad, and the Downright Ugly: What Not to Do to Be an Effective Leader*, Dr. Joey Beeson provides the reader with illustrations of various types of leaders. While leadership texts are replete with practical and theoretical examples, the noteworthy components in this book are that Dr. Beeson provides the reader with challenges to status quo definitions. His use of common terminology to describe the characteristics is highlighted with a continual reminder of how one's moral compass needs to encapsulate ethical and principled-based leadership in the multiple roles, functions, and dynamics of leaders.

The text is not intended to provide the reader with theoretical constructs; this engaging series of examples from recent doctoral leadership students provides quality, insightful, and realistic perspectives. Practitioners and researchers should use these examples as they provide a framework for what has/is being experienced in leadership roles in their profession. They are heartfelt and immersive views that present the reader with the current state of leadership studies.

Other aspects of this text include a comprehensive summary of leadership characteristics and qualities, both good and bad. Without casting aspersions to individual situations and types of leaders, these writings detail not just a handbook of "dos and don'ts" but rather challenge the reader to complete a reflective approach to one's styles and to provide impetus to translating these thoughts and ideas into actions which are purposeful, thoughtful, and moral.

The final components of this text provide examples of how the various characters in leadership harmed and moved the areas of their responsibilities to one of what some would call unethical, immoral, or demeaning actions. The uniqueness of this text stays focused on Scriptural details, not so much to proselytize, but to urge the reader to reflect on the actions of others and themselves in following the moral compass provided in Scripture.

Dr. Beeson's extensive leadership roles in various institutions, his engaging connection to students of leadership studies, and his deep-seated adherence to Scripture and following the example of the Master Leader all identify this text as an emerging opportunity for instructors, students, and peers to "respect," that is to look at again, their own personal journeys and how to consider adapting and adopting the golden rule in life's journey. Through his classroom experiences, multiple administrative roles, and ongoing faith journey, Dr. Beeson's practical, thoughtful, and informed writings provide the reader with thoughtful reflections and principled-based situational analysis to guide, build, and unify leaders toward an ethical and moral code of conduct.

I believe in Dr. Beeson – his values, Christ-centered approach to the truth, and wanting to provide future and current leaders with honest and realistic information. Dr. Beeson's perspectives are from a shared interest in the truth. Joey Beeson is a man of faith, integrity, and great insights who details how leaders can be influential and emulate goodness and the beauty of servant-based leadership.

It is an honor and privilege to support the publication of this book. May it be used in your life and for kingdom purposes.

Enjoy and learn from it!
George W. Metz, PhD

ACKNOWLEDGMENTS

Thank you to the many anonymous contributors to this book. Regardless of how much or how little you shared and allowed me to pass along in this book, your stories let this book go from being a dream, idea, and concept into a published reality. You know who you are, and I thank you from the bottom of my heart!

Next, a very special thanks is owed to Dr. Karen Stewart, Dr. Courtney Creech, Dr. Abbie Scott, and Dr. and Lt. Col. Kimberly Champagne. Thank you for allowing me to be a part of your writing journey in your doctoral program, and with this book, returning the favor of being a part of my writing journey.

Next, thank you to the wonderfully talented Sebastian Catangay, who illustrated the images in this book. Though only an eighth grader at the time of publication, he is positioned to go places in life with his talents in art and music!

Next, to my team at WestBow Press. Thank you for your guidance and support in helping me publish my first book!

Next, thank you to the incredible, godly leaders who have had a positive impact on my life up to this point – Joe Beeson (yes, my awesome dad), Greg Kurtz, Barry Bennett, Stephanie Shafer, Steve Stark, Joe Hale, Debbie MacCullough, Paula Gossard, Sheryl Vasso, Laura McCollum, Brian Toews, Brenda Mellon, George Metz, Kathy Sobolewski,

William Ross, Jim Spencer, Kylon Middleton, and more. May God continue to use you for His Kingdom!

Finally, I acknowledge and thank my Creator, Lord, and Savior, Jesus Christ, for what He has allowed my family and me to experience past, present, and future. To Him be all the glory, and thank you, Jesus, for never leaving or forsaking me!

Before we start this journey of exploring what not to do to be an effective leader, here are some initial quotes on bad leadership to get you thinking about the topic. They were compiled by Emily May at the Niagara Institute (2022).

- "Bad leaders believe their team works for them. Great leaders believe they work for their team." - Alexander den Heijer, Motivational Speaker
- "When you were made a leader, you weren't given a crown, you were given the responsibility to bring out the best in others." - Jack Welch, Former CEO of General Electric
- "It doesn't make sense to hire smart people and then tell them what to do. We hire smart people so they can tell us what to do.'" - Steve Jobs, Co-Founder of Apple
- "Bad leaders care about who is right. Good leaders care about what is right.'" - Simon Sinek, Author, and Motivational Speaker
- "Leadership is about solving problems. The day employees stop bringing you their problems is the day you have stopped leading them. They have either lost confidence that you can help or conclude you do not care. Either case is a failure on leadership." - Colin Powell, Politician

- "Leadership is not a popularity contest; it's about leaving your ego at the door. The name of the game is to lead without a title." - Robin S. Sharma, Lawyer and Author
- "A strong secure leader accepts blame and gives credit. A weak insecure leader gives blame and takes credit." - John Wooden, Basketball Coach
- "You can tell a bully from a leader by how they treat people who disagree with them." - Miles K. Davis, President of Linfield College

Contrast the quotes above with the verses below from Psalm 118, filled with unique statements about God, who He is, and what He does. This passage is a constant source of encouragement and comfort, especially during seasons of difficulty. As you begin reading this book, may you be blessed by the selected verses of this psalm, with emphasis added through italics and brackets. Also, both with this passage below and throughout this book, the English Standard Version (ESV) of the Bible is used for all references unless otherwise noted.

5 Out of my distress, I called on the LORD;
the LORD answered me and set me free.

6 *The LORD is on my side*; I will not
fear. *What can man do to me?*

7 *The LORD is on my side* as my helper; I shall
look in triumph on those who hate me.

8 It is better to take *refuge in the
LORD* than to trust in man.

⁹ It is better to take *refuge in the LORD* than to
trust in princes [or those in leadership] …

¹³ I was pushed hard so that I was
falling, *but the Lord helped me.*

¹⁴ *The Lord is my strength* and my song;
he has become my salvation…

²⁸ You are my God, and *I will give thanks to
you*; you are my God; I will extol you.

²⁹ Oh give thanks to the Lord, *for he is good*;
for his steadfast love endures forever!

CHAPTER ONE

HOW THIS BOOK CAME TO FRUITION

OPENING THOUGHTS TO PONDER

While the inspiration for this book started as a cathartic and therapeutic activity, I quickly realized in conversations with other leaders from a variety of contexts that many in leadership positions (and many not in these positions) have experienced the not-so-good, the bad, and the downright ugly in the workplace. Most of us have likely been hurt, burned, and mistreated. Potentially, you have been a part of the giving end versus only the receiving end of bad leadership. No sane person wakes up one day and thinks or says things like...

- "I want to work for a cruel boss that treats me poorly," or
- "I want to work for a company or organization that lacks character, morals, or ethics," or
- "I wish I could have an employer that is so toxic and hostile that I will need to seek mental and physical help and healing," or

- "I want to relocate my family to a new job that will implode and make my personal and family life miserable."

Sadly, bad leaders are everywhere. Yes, some leaders are bad because they intentionally, for whatever reason or reasons, seem to be thrilled by ruining the lives of others for their gain. Some leaders are bad because they are narcissistic and only care about themselves and what "I do." Some leaders are bad because they have poor interpersonal skills or have little to no self-efficacy. Some leaders are bad because they do not care about the people working for them; they only care about the bottom line and results. Some leaders are bad because they intentionally choose to be unteachable or receive constructive criticism from others about improving.

From a Biblical perspective, we are flawed, imperfect, messed up, in need of change and redemption, and have fallen short of God's glory and standard (Romans 3:23). Scripture teaches the very core of who we are is depraved, self-seeking, discontented, and yes, whether we like to admit it or not, evil. Even amidst the heart change available through knowing Christ, we still have old-self tendencies, habits, routines, and proclivities that can easily creep up and entangle our souls. These old tendencies can even make the best of Christians end up being bad leaders. Some of us have worked for nonbelievers who have mistreated us, and it should not surprise us that they do not lead like Christ because they do not know Christ. They have not undergone the extraordinary heart change that can and should change how they view others and themselves. Then, we may have to admit another grim reality – some of us have sadly worked for believers, or at least so-called believers (or Christians in name only) who treated us worse than nonbelievers. These experiences are not only damaging to us, but the reputation of God's kingdom and the name of Christ are marred as a result of their poor leadership.

While this book contains experiences and stories of leadership, let me be clear regarding a foundational truth. Scripture teaches that everyone has been created and made in the image of God. It also teaches that we are fallen, sinful, and doomed to an eternal separation from our Creator. We cannot be good enough to earn God's favor, and the only way to change our eternal destiny and present condition is through having a relationship with Jesus. He is THE one and only way, truth, and life (John 14:6). As a result of the opportunity for a heart change in knowing and following Jesus, there are three categories of people, and for this book, three categories of leaders. This book is for you regardless of your category or the leader you currently work for.

THE THREE CATEGORIES OF LEADERS

These three categories of leaders exist in our homes, offices, churches, and communities, and it is my prayer that you either already fall into category three below or you deeply consider choosing to be in this category:

Category 1 - Nonbelievers, Non-Christians

Some leaders have not yet chosen to commit their lives to Jesus; as a result, they do not seek to follow and honor Him with their lives, affecting not only who they are as individuals but also how they lead. This book describes this first leader category as nonbelievers, non-Christians, pre-believers, or pre-Christians.

Category 2 – Christians in Name Only

Some leaders claim to know Christ but are either Christians in name only or are not walking in a manner worthy of the gospel (Ephesians 4:1). These leaders may be young Christians who are new in their faith and still learning what it means to live differently. These leaders may be Christians in a season of struggle, whereby their faith and relationship with God are stagnant or dry, and no evidence of a life with Christ is on display for others as they lead. These leaders may be choosing not to grow in their faith in Christ, and as a result, their old-self tendencies quickly take over, causing them to be miserable in their walk with God and how they lead and treat others. The beauty of the gospel and this book is that it is the heart of God for all to know Him and to live for Him, and we as leaders, though imperfect, choose to either have a positive effect on the lives of others we lead or a destructive effect. In this book, the term Christian in name only is used to describe this second category of leader.

Category 3 – Believers, Christians

Some leaders have chosen to accept, believe, and follow Jesus, and as a result, this heart and life change that occurs from knowing Jesus visibly looks different in how they live and lead. Scripture repetitively reminds a believer of the importance of bearing good fruit. These leaders are imperfect, but they choose to yield their lives and leadership actions to Christ. The Apostle Paul wrote in Galatians 5:22-23 that a person who follows Jesus seeks to imitate Jesus and is marked by a life that demonstrates and is evidenced by "love, joy, peace, patience, kindness, goodness, faithfulness, gentleness, and self-control." In the same chapter in Galatians, Paul urges us to "not become conceited, provoking one another, envying one another." Again, I would be remiss not to tell you about the fantastic life available through knowing and following Jesus. In this book, believers and Christians describe this third leader category.

A JOURNEY OF HARD AND DIFFICULT

In the Summer of 2020, during the global COVID-19 pandemic, I relocated my family to what seemed to be my dream job. Before this move, we lived in various places as a family (Southeast Asia, Mississippi, New Jersey, and Pennsylvania). Before marriage, I had lived in multiple places (South Carolina, Oklahoma, Ohio, and Texas). The move was an opportunity for a fresh start after being betrayed and burned by leadership in an organization where I served for nearly a decade and where my children spent many of their critical formative years.

With high hopes and renewed optimism, we made this move, thinking that things could not be worse in the workplace than what we left in our previous locale. Within six months, what started as a fantastic job with the most incredible colleagues and customers to serve began to take a noticeable turn. Then, within less than a year, things began to shift dramatically. As John Maxwell once famously said, "Everything rises and falls on leadership" (Colvin, 2021). Wow, my colleagues, customers, and I were in for a wild ride as the organization began to implode.

Within less than a year, the place did not look or feel the same, and one common reason resonated with the organization's employees and customers. There was a systemic problem with the organization's leadership. What seemed to be such a promising opportunity with this organization in being positioned for growth, impact, and legacy suddenly and dramatically shifted into a downward spiral of bad communication, little to no transparency, lashing out, unethical decision-making, yelling, threats, and seeking to sweep everything under the proverbial rug. Employees and customers were left asking the question: was the leadership of this organization either so poor and ineffective that they did not know better, or were they strategically seeking to destroy the organization and leave a wake of destruction with the mistreatment of employees and customers?

THE GOAL OF THIS BOOK

In 2004, and then again in 2011 with a revised and expanded edition, Dr. John Hoover published a book entitled *How to Work for an Idiot: Revised & Expanded with More Idiots, More Insanity, and More Incompetency: Survive and Thrive Without Killing Your Boss*. In the Introduction, Dr. Hoover wrote, "This book contains the debris they scraped off the walls after my head exploded. For years, I wrote books on leadership, creativity, and organizational performance...My clients welcomed me and nodded approvingly as I taught the principles of teamwork and open communication. They even waited politely until I had finished and left the building before ignoring my advice. *How to Work for an Idiot is my revenge* [emphasis added] (Hoover, 2011, p. 9).

Dear reader, it can be pretty easy to feel and experience what Dr. Hoover described in his book's Introduction provided in the previous paragraph if you live long enough and work long enough. A new boss may be hired, and then everything will worsen. You will have to consciously choose not to be overcome by the bubbling up of negative emotions inside due to the mistreatment of others by those in leadership. Anger, revenge, and retribution will not solve the problem of poor leadership, though it might feel good to consider these negative emotions for a moment. Instead, as Dr. Hoover and Scripture tell us, the ultimate reality of the issue is a heart problem, and a remedy is needed and available.

Here are some quick considerations as we start the journey of this book:

- Can a nonbeliever be a good leader? Yes! This is evidenced through personal experience and the many voices who contributed to this book.
- Can a nonbeliever be a bad leader? Yes!
- Can a Christian be a good leader? Yes!
- Can a Christian be a bad leader? Yes!

All leaders can be good, and most leaders have had plenty of training opportunities to gain experience on how to be effective, and then the addition of experience to tell and guide them to what it means to be a good leader. Plenty of excellent books and articles have been published about what to do to be an effective, good leader (books by Maxwell, Collins, Kerr, Hoover, etc.). Scripture gives us a wonderful picture of this topic, which will be explored in this book.

But let us consider something that is crucial and an overwhelming theme of this book by taking a moment to reflect on the following two questions:

- What can we learn from our personal experiences and hearing others' stories of what not to do to be an effective, good leader?
- What if leaders were to consider and value the stories of what to avoid, what not to do, how not to be hated, and how not to destroy a team or organization?

REFLECT HERE...

These two questions and considerations have formed this book's goal and purpose. This book is *not* a revenge tour, though there may be reasons for it to be so. Again, I want to reiterate the previous sentence. This book is *not* a revenge tour. Instead, in a lighthearted way, and at times in some heavyhearted ways, this book has collected and provided principles and stories of what to do to avoid being an ineffective, bad leader. The book draws upon history, Scripture, and personal experiences by offering insights into what to avoid or not do if you want to be a great leader.

Sadly, many who will read this book realize they, too, have experienced in part or whole what is captured in the following pages. Take heart, dear reader – you are not alone in what you have experienced, and rather than make this book a comparison activity of whether you have experienced worse situations with leadership or not, look for the learning opportunities contained within each chapter and contributed story. Though we may struggle (past, present, and future) in our employment for many reasons, experience can be a great teacher, even when it is a negative experience. If nothing else, we learn what not to do. Or, when we observe or experience someone in leadership do something destructive, we say and commit to practice that I will never do that when I have opportunities to lead others.

ESSENTIAL QUESTIONS TO ASK

While this book is not necessarily meant to be a traditional workbook or textbook, intentional opportunities and space are provided to pause, reflect, and write. Depending on your season of life, it may be beneficial to do more than read this book; you are invited to use the prompts to brainstorm, journal, and write. Also, it can be pretty easy to "armchair quarterback" the situations and stories in this book with what could have or should have been done. I encourage you to honestly insert yourself into situations as you reflect and potentially write.

The following three essential questions are considered throughout this book. As you encounter each chapter and the principles, characteristics, and stories contained therein, you are encouraged to take the time to work through them:

1. How would you have handled the situation?
2. How could the situation have been handled differently?
3. And most importantly, what can be learned from the situation?

Each story in this book is based on authentic experiences. Some contributions to the book were a sentence or two, and some were much longer; however, again, the intent is not to throw people directly under the bus, so great care has been taken to protect the identity of individuals and specific companies. Pseudonyms are intentionally used. Company and organization names are omitted, too.

The other reality of this book is that when another person wrongs us, especially in leadership or authority, there is that natural innate tendency to react. Again, this, too, is not the goal of this book. Regardless of how we define and categorize leadership and what the experts say about leadership, we are all on a journey, especially if you are a Christ follower. We hold on to two essential truths. First, we know that God works out everything for the good and according to His plan (Romans 8:28), and second, we know that troubles and tests assist us with endurance and maturity in our faith journey (James 1:2-4).

A QUICK OVERVIEW OF THE FIVE BAD LEADERSHIP CHARACTERS

The next thing to note about this book is how it is organized. First, time is spent reviewing the characteristics of an effective, godly leader, and the voices and perspectives of Scripture are intentionally considered. Then, this book shifts to situations, responses to prompts, and personal stories. The stories shared in this book will no doubt show the negative characteristics of leaders, but you will note that the stories are organized among five leadership characters.

Each of these leadership characters is generally defined below, and note, that it is likely that bad, ineffective leaders, regardless of the three categories of leaders previously considered, likely share the characteristics of more than one of the leadership characters explained below.

The Vile Witch

These leaders are typically more toward the top of the leadership hierarchy but can also be found in middle-level management. They seem to do everything possible to "I'll get you my pretty," like Elphaba, one of the wicked witches from the book *Wicked: The Life and Times of the Wicked Witch of the West (Wicked Years, 1)*, or the film, *The Wonderful Wizard of Oz* (MacGuire, 2000). They could care less about anyone's needs under them. They do not listen, model next to nothing positive, feel threatened by anyone who asks questions, throw their

weight around like a Machiavellian bull in a china shop, harasses employees through intimidation, yell to be heard and get their way, stand over others with a wagging finger, and are paranoid that someone might expose their lack of character, skills, and ethics.

The Suck-Up Lapdog

These leaders are typically in middle-level management, and to stay in their position, they usually surrender their soul and well-being to a Vile Witch, Shady Sleaze, or Pontius Pilate Sideliner-type leader above them. Rather than providing care and support for those under them, they only care about pleasing and doing their boss's wishes. Their soul is sold to evil, and they have little to no established trust with others working for/with them because their only concern is to keep the boss happy. This leader may be clueless about their job responsibilities, but because of the constant suck-up to their boss, job security never seems to be a concern.

The "Oh No!" I Am in Over My Head.

These leaders typically have no idea how to lead or think they know what they are doing when they do not. They can be found at all levels of management. They possess little to no evidence, skill, or experience of knowing how to lead, build a team or community, or buy in, and it is evident to everyone except them that they are clearly in over their head for the job. They somehow have created an aura around them that they believe they know what they are doing when they have no clue. They are often poor communicators, get upset when questions come, and try to hide from others, especially those working under them, so their ineffectiveness cannot be discovered.

The Shady Sleaze

These leaders creep out everyone except those lucky or disillusioned enough to be in their inner circle. They, too, can be found at all levels of management. Somehow, they feel they are above the law, the rules and institutional policies do not apply to them, and they can do whatever they wish. They

blur the lines of morals, ethics, and the rule of law. They only care about creepily creating an inner circle of loyalty through whatever means, ethically or not, and intentionally create an "us versus them" mentality in an organization. They hide behind mistruths and pretend to be genuine when, in fact, they are one step away from corruption, scandal, or indictment (or possibly are already on the way to these devastating ends but have not yet been unmasked).

The Pontius Pilate Sideliner

These leaders typically know what is going on in an organization and may even be attuned to the pulse and culture of the concerns and issues within the organization; however, rather than choosing to step in to be a positive solution to provide support and help to employees and customers, these leaders sadly stay on the sideline and do not actively get involved. They are often found toward the top of the leadership hierarchy. As the Roman leader of this name did, when having the power to release Jesus because

he found no fault or wrong in Jesus, these leaders washed their hands of any sticky or challenging situations they encountered. They often place too much blind trust in the ineffective leaders working under them, possibly because they do not care or are so nonconfrontational that they are frightened by others or situations that may be threatening or challenging. They knowingly allow those in leadership to do whatever they wish, and they have little to no commitment to accountability and responsibility. At times, these leaders leave an organization, and the wake of destruction is then fully realized after their departure, and the organization is left to clean up the mess.

FINAL REMINDERS

As we close out this first chapter, I implore you to remember the goal of this book. Regardless of the category of person from earlier in this chapter, everyone you have or ever will work for is a flawed, imperfect human being. We will be disappointed by others, including those in leadership. We may even be mistreated, betrayed, and outright persecuted by leaders, even by those who are supposed to be Christ's followers. And, let us be honest: in our leadership positions, we have made mistakes, too. Nevertheless, God can and will use these people, circumstances, and experiences, even the negative ones, to help us grow and develop our faith and leadership skills. In the next chapter, we consider the application of leadership theories, presence, and influence.

REFLECT HERE ON CHAPTER THOUGHTS,
REACTIONS, RESPONSES, ACTION ITEMS...

CHAPTER TWO

LEADERSHIP THEORIES, PRESENCE, AND INFLUENCE

While the goal of this book is not intentionally meant to be heavily theoretical or philosophical, leaders, whether knowingly or not, have been shaped somehow. Their training may have been in a classroom or professional development sessions. It may have been some on-the-job training with orientation and a hands-on, apprenticeship-type approach. It may have been the approach of here you go, best of luck to you, and see you later. Regardless of the amount or quality of training provided, you have been formally or informally trained in how to lead.

THEY ARE EVERYWHERE, THEY ARE EVERYWHERE!

We do not have to look very far to see leaders around us. We find them in our homes, our places of employment, our neighborhoods, the places we eat and shop, our churches, and our places of government. We see them on television, phones, computers, tablets, and in person. They are found in our living rooms, at our kitchen tables, in offices, in conference rooms, at working lunches, in conferences and seminars, in community meetings, in classrooms, in auditoriums, and more. We have developed ideas about how they should act and treat their followers. We have opinions about needing them to be held accountable for their choices, and we are watching them to see how they use their position and authority to impact and influence.

When I taught leadership courses at both the master's and doctoral levels, one of the early considerations related to leadership included brainstorming the numerous people in various contexts who have had some authority or oversight over our lives. This could include but is not limited to our parents, older family members, pastors, community leaders, law enforcement officials, politicians, presidents, executive officers, immediate supervisors, mid-level managers, and more.

The brainstorming that we conducted in these courses was also personalized. My students were encouraged to think through their own lives, as God has placed them in positions of leadership and authority, too. These places are likely found at home, work, church, and community. Before you continue with the next section of this chapter, take a moment to reflect on the various positions and roles you currently possess and those you have held in your past.

REFLECT HERE...

LEADERSHIP THEORIES AND APPLICATIONS

Regardless of a leader's training and experience, it is likely that they are operating out of one or more of the prevailing categories of leadership theory. Peter Northouse's book, *Leadership Theory and Practice*, presented "an academically robust account of the major theories and models of leadership with a focus on how theory can inform practice. Northouse uses a consistent structure for each chapter, allowing readers to compare and contrast theories easily. Case studies and questionnaires provide students practical examples and opportunities to deepen their understanding of their leadership style" (Sage, 2023).

In his book, Northouse defined and described leadership and then provided a glimpse at the approaches to leadership, including a leader's traits, skills, behaviors, and situational contexts. He also described and evaluated the following leadership theories: path-goal, leader-member exchange, transformational, authentic, servant, adaptive, and inclusive. He ended his book by looking at followership, ethics, and team building.

Rather than focus on theories for theory's sake, two applications of leadership theories heavily influenced by Northouse's work are provided below. Additionally, these two applications are story-driven, which fits within the intended approach of this book. These two applications of leadership theory come from two of my former doctoral students, whom I had the privilege to teach and guide through their dissertation journey. So, thank you, Dr. Courtney Creech and Dr. Abbie Scott, for your permission to share your thoughts below and give insights into how leadership theories are applied in practice. Note: their work comes from their document submission for the summative course assessment in their doctoral program's leadership theory course.

Theory Application #1 - Dr. Creech

Leadership is hard to define. Researchers have worked for years to produce a definition encompassing all a leader is and does. I started teaching in 2004, and when I think of being a leader and my elements of leadership, I think of my time as a classroom teacher and my involvement in my church. I am a Christian; I have morals and values that govern and affect everything I do. As a child of God, I know who I am; I care about putting others first and doing what is right, moral, and ethical, regardless of the situation. God called me to this program to help me develop as a leader. The styles of leadership that I identify with at this point in my career are authentic, transformational, and servant leadership. At this point, I strive to be an authentic transformational servant leader.

I am authentic; I am true to who I am. I grew up in a Christian home and learned early to do what is right. I have always had a true definition of what is right and what is wrong. I continue to look to Jesus in all I do; he is my true north, the center of my moral compass, and the head of my household. I believe in being transformational; I want to improve the world for my children and those I teach. You can count on me to do what is proper and ethical while trying to make a change. As a servant leader, I strive to put the needs of others first, live by the golden rule, and try to teach others to do the same. "Except for servant, transformational, and authentic leadership, none of the other theories discussed in this book focuses on the role of ethics in the leadership process" (Northouse, 2019, p. 352). Leadership is about influencing others; it is not something I could demonstrate without showing my values or being true to who I am, leaning on and looking to my true north, Jesus.

The style I identify most with is Authentic Leadership. Authentic leaders understand their values and conduct themselves based on these values. As an authentic leader, I keep Jesus as the center of my life; he is the head of our household. Even in different situations, I still hold on to who I am. When I respond or react to different situations, my character remains true. George identifies five characteristics of authentic leadership: "(1) They have a strong sense of purpose, (2) they have strong values about the right thing to do, (3) they establish trusting relationships with others, (4) they demonstrate self-discipline and act on their values, and (5) they are sensitive and empathetic to the plight of others" (Northouse, 2019, p.199). Authentic leaders know their purpose and are inspired and motivated about their goals. Setting goals is a big part of who I am as a person. I am intrinsically motivated to accomplish whatever I set out to do. I enjoy setting goals for things I want to achieve. Earning a doctoral degree is a goal I set for myself fifteen years ago.

Authentic leaders focus on and develop relationships with others. Creating and building relationships has always been something I value. As a classroom teacher, I spend most of my time and energy building relationships with my students. I spend the first several weeks of a new school year getting to know the students personally. I foster and continue to grow student-teacher relationships by holding community meetings in the classroom. I also make it a priority for my students to attend extracurricular events outside of school. I attended baseball and basketball games, piano and dance recitals, and a church baptism this school year. I also take time to meet and conference with parents because parent-teacher communication and relationships are essential. My students know if they ever need something, they can come to me and count on me, even if I am no longer their teacher.

Relationships are an essential part of who I am outside of the classroom. As a member of my church, a small group leader, and a member of the finance committee, I value my relationships with the other church members, my small group, and the finance committee members. My husband and I lead a small group at our home each week. We have developed relationships with the people in our group. We can depend on one another when life gets busy and overwhelming. Our church finance team has a shared vision, and we have established trusting relationships. Our team works together to make decisions that will affect the future of our church. I also believe having solid relationships with my coworkers is essential. I attend retirement celebrations, teacher of the year programs, and fellowship events with my coworkers to foster strong relationships. Having genuine relationships with people and getting to know them is a big part of who I am, and relationships are a big part of authentic leadership.

Another dimension of authentic leadership is self-discipline; this quality helps leaders reach their goals. As a self-starter, I like to get things done and not wait until the last minute. I have learned how to manage my time when tasks pile up. Getting up early, staying up late, whatever I need to do to get the job done. College was easy because I was self-disciplined; I would not go out or do other things until my work was complete. I am the same way as a classroom teacher. One of my colleagues said she thinks I have a "magic wand" to get things done. I do not waste time; I like to figure out all the details and plan to do a job or a task once and correctly. I know being self-disciplined will help me when it comes to completing this program.

The second element of leadership that I identify with is transformational leadership. "Transformational leadership is a process that changes and transforms people. It is concerned with emotions, values, ethics, standards, and long-term goals" (Northouse, 2019, p. 163). A transformational leader is attentive to the needs and motives of followers. Transformational leaders are concerned with change. Wicker-Miurin talked about change and said, "We can't keep doing what we've always done because we'll get the same results we've always gotten" (TED Talk, 2009). Transformational leaders help followers reach their fullest potential. Bass (1985) developed four factors in transformational leadership: idealized influence or charisma, inspirational motivation, intellectual stimulation, and individualized consideration (Northouse, 2019, p. 168). Transformational leadership provides a broad set of generalizations of behaviors and actions typical of transformational leaders. These behaviors include empowering and nurturing followers in change, having moral values, exhibiting confidence and competence, being articulate and able to express strong ideals, creating and communicating a shared vision of the organization, encouraging others, and celebrating their accomplishments. As a classroom teacher, I have some of the characteristics exhibited by transformational leaders.

I have taught the System Z program at my school for the past three years. This program, designed for third-grade students failing to meet grade-level reading expectations, provides fluency and decoding strategies for struggling readers. This teaching position is not an easy one to take on; some teachers at our school compare it to mission work. The other schools in our district run the program as a "pull-out" program because they have Title I funding that our school does not receive. My ultimate goal is to motivate and empower the children in my classroom. I work with students to set goals and develop new strategies for reading so they can close the gap on their deficiencies in reading. Some students find out that they have learning disabilities in reading, but through learning new strategies and encouraging students, students become confident and empowered. According to Northouse (2019), transformational leaders effectively motivate followers.

Most recently, I taught one of my school's Gifted and Talented groups. One of the characteristics of gifted and talented people is that they can be underachievers. I had to motivate and inspire them to see value in their work. I had to make what we were learning in class exciting and appealing. I did this by letting the students pick points of interest to research. I also booked time in our STEAM (Science,

Technology, Engineering, Arts, and Mathematics) lab to provide intellectual stimulation. In the STEAM lab, students use creativity and innovation to work through challenging tasks. According to Northouse (2019), transformational leaders have high expectations for followers; they have confidence in followers' abilities to meet expectations.

Transformational leaders create a connection with followers, just as teachers do with students. According to Hemerling, leaders must be inclusive and prioritize people (TED Talk, 2016). Transformational leaders are good role models both in and out of the classroom. They have a high standard of moral and ethical conduct. I live in the community I teach in; I often see my students at church, restaurants, and shopping. I need to set a good example for them; I want my students and others to know that they can count on me to do what is right. Treating others with kindness and compassion is something I hope my students see through my actions. I want them to put the needs of others above their own. Our school motto this year was "Change the World for Good." I want my students to know that even as children, they can change the world by their actions and how they treat others, learning to put others first. In our classroom this year, we collected school supplies for Low Country Orphan Relief, raised money for Relay for Life, and collected food and toys for Sinbad and Sadie Second Chace Rescue. As a teacher, modeling community service is essential to my job.

Additionally, in the classroom, I like students to see how much they have grown over the school year. One way I do this is by creating growth charts. At the start of the school year, students complete the Reading Inventory. This online assessment gives students a Lexile score (reading level). Students can use this to help find books that are "just right" for them to read (not too easy, not too tricky). The growth chart that we create helps students track their progress on the Reading Inventory throughout the school year. Students take the assessment three or four times during the year. I use this chart to encourage and celebrate students. Students can see their growth throughout the school year, and they can see the time they spend reading both in and outside of the classroom setting pays off. Encouraging and celebrating my students is one of my favorite parts of my job as a teacher.

The final element of leadership I identify with now is servant leadership. Servant leaders are leaders who put followers first. A servant leader is a leader and a servant at the same time. They demonstrate strong moral behavior. Servant leadership focuses on the behaviors leaders should do to put followers first and support the personal development of the followers. This is the only leadership approach that frames leadership around caring for others. "The description of a servant leader reads very much like the job description for an educator: being committed to putting one's followers first, being honest with them and treating them fairly, and making it a priority to listen to them and their abilities, needs, and goals, which, in turn, allows these followers to achieve their full potential." (Northouse, 2019, p. 95). I know as a teacher, I am a servant leader. Jesus was the ultimate servant leader, and he showed this leadership not by the words he spoke but through his actions.

Spears (2002) identified ten characteristics of servant leadership in Greenleaf's writing. The characteristics are as follows: listening, empathy, healing, awareness, persuasion, conceptualization, foresight, stewardship, commitment to the growth of people, and building community (Greenleaf, 1977, p. 229). As a teacher, I display these characteristics in and out of the classroom. Listening to my students is something that I place value in because I want them to have a voice in the classroom and their community—showing empathy for and towards my students by trying to see things from their point of view and trying to teach them to think of how others in the same situation may feel. When I address behavior concerns, I try to have the student step back and think of the situation from another perspective. Teaching students empathy and empathy for others is vital. As a servant leader, I care about the personal well-being of my students (healing). Caring for the whole student takes time and effort. I am concerned not only about academic growth but also for the well-being of my students. As I mentioned above, I am committed to student progress and growth. I look at data and test results and listen to student feedback to plan direct instruction groups for my students to ensure that I meet their needs. Building a classroom community is extremely important to me. I try to create an atmosphere where students feel safe, valued, and connected. I focus on my students when I think of myself as a servant leader and trying to be more like Jesus. It is not about me; it is about them. Heyler and Martin (2018), "The servant leader sees subordinates, or followers, as the main reason for being in the position and wants to do everything in his/her power to ensure they grow" (p. 231).

To conclude, at this point in my life, I have some of the characteristics associated with authentic, transformational, and servant leadership. Participating in this program is part of God's plan for me. As I continue to develop as a leader and learn more through the doctoral program, my views on leadership may change. Northouse (2019) notes the underrepresentation of women in significant leadership positions. Upon completing my doctoral program, I could help catalyze change in gender equality in leadership roles.

Pause for a moment and reflect on Dr. Creech's applications of leadership theory. What stood out and resonated with you? What points do you agree with? What points do you disagree with? What statements could use further investigation for your leadership development?

REFLECT HERE...

Theory Application #2 - Dr. Scott

Leadership is far more than the group of letters found next to an individual's name indicating the level they have risen in an organization. In many cases, the true leaders within an organization are not even the individuals with the recognizable letters of success plastered on business cards, desk placards, or office nameplates. Leaders must recognize their role in an organization and understand their impact on the people who are responsible for their successes because, without followers, leaders do not even exist.

The ambiguous nature of defining what leadership is and what it is not allows the study of it to be arduous, contradictory, inundated with opinions, and, honestly, confusing. So many approaches claim to be the guiding principle for success; it is easy to guess one's leadership style second if only one can be selected. Many leadership theories borrow from each other, so I find it difficult not to utilize several approaches when quantifying my exact leadership style. Despite the overlapping of strategies, as long as I, as a leader, remain faithful to a moral ideal with intentions to stay ethical, multiple leadership styles may be incorporated to reach both personal and professional success.

The idea of the moral compass is central to any leadership discussion. Morality in leadership is seen through what a leader does and who the leader is at the core of their character (Northouse, 2019, p. 337). A leader's ethical nature guides their decisions, which creates the path down which an organization and its members travel. Ethical leadership is defined by Brown, Trevino, and Harrison (2005) as "...the demonstration of normatively appropriate conduct through personal actions and interpersonal relationships, and the promotion of such conduct to followers through two-way communication, reinforcement, and decision-making" (p. 120). While it is true that not all people who become leaders act ethically (history has more than taught us this), it can be said that truly great leaders work through a personal lens of morality and require their organization to do the same.

Much of my moral compass revolves around equality: gender, race, religion, socio-economic status, etc. I can thank my mother for my current moral compass because she taught me to treat people equally and respectfully. It was (and still is) a requirement in my household. I am a product of Northouse's (2019) idea, claiming, "When practiced over time, from youth to adulthood, good values become habitual, and part of the people themselves" (p. 341). My morality concerning equality is more than a habit; therefore, as a leader, equality is not something I will let go of because it is very much a part of my being. On paper, most organizations claim to abide by rules prohibiting discrimination, going as far as having training, distributing memos, and holding meetings (what I view as actions) to ensure this. However, in my experience, many leaders' actions are not backed up by their words or the words they allow to be said.

As a leader, my followers and other leaders in my organization must witness me utilizing my moral compass to lead in both action and words. I must walk the walk and talk the talk to demonstrate the ethical lens through which I desire to lead. Walking the walk seems to get more emphasis than talking the talk because actions are thought to speak so much louder than words, but I believe the words a person says deserve as much, if not more, attention.

I work in a place that does this each year at the beginning of the year regarding students' backgrounds and individuality. Our leader gets one of the teachers to run through a PowerPoint presentation defining and describing students and how to help them while she sits in the audience and adds nothing to the conversation. Many teachers are reluctant to listen to anything about either population because of their personal beliefs and make it known by ignoring what is being presented and making snide comments to their neighbors. Furthermore, each year as the yearbook adviser, I advocate for a "neutral" option for students to utilize for the formal yearbook picture, and each year, I am told this is not an option because "We are not doing that here." This confuses me because we hold meetings about acceptance, yet her words do not support her disingenuous actions.

To circumvent the issue, I find it unethical to utilize casual photos where students can choose an outfit. My ethical responsibility is to be with the students in the school and accommodate them while not going against my leader. As Northouse (2019) explained, "Ethics is central to leadership, and leaders help to establish and reinforce organizational values" (p. 342). A leader's job is to consistently act ethically so that the followers do the same. In my place of work, it is obvious the leader's moral compass regarding this issue is not taken seriously because hardly any emphasis is placed on the follow-through required to impact the environment positively. Suppose a leader's moral compass is not accurate. In that case, the organization will not be able to act ethically because followers will see right through the act, and eventually, the facade will crumble.

Over the last few years, much notice has been

served regarding language and workplace behavior. The #MeToo Movement is a perfect example of a fake moral compass eventually causing the crash and burn of people and even entire organizations because of the lack of an accurate moral compass. Brzezinski (2018) explained, "From Hollywood to Congress, to major media companies, powerful men are facing professional consequences for their mistreatment of less powerful employees, mentees and admirers" (para. 1). Clearly, many individuals' actions are called into question when discussing the #MeToo Movement, but very often what made so many followers uncomfortable initially were never addressed inappropriate comments made by both leaders and followers. Eventually, these words lead to actions because allowing the words to be said with no consequence caused the affected to have no power.

My moral compass is seen in my classroom because I create a safe space within it to help combat the negative impact words can have. My students are aware of what is expected, and I am up-front about why it is important to me because "...moral humility exhibited by leaders will ultimately influence the moral behavior of followers" (Owens, Yam, Bednar, Mao, & Hart, 2019, p. 149). I have witnessed students enter my classroom believing it is acceptable to address others negatively and leave it understanding how to treat another person. As a leader, I may not entirely change people, but I can influence how they treat each other and ultimately make each other feel.

My moral compass and how it relates to my leadership is pretty simple: I must treat everyone in the organization as humans and require my fellow leaders and followers to do the same. I recognize that ethics in leadership is a more significant issue than what seems to be the idea of respect I have harped on, but it is the issue I find to be the most impactful. Ethical leaders must consider so many choices and decisions that are not about respect and can easily stray from a moral compass regarding those choices; however, the most significant impact a leader can have on their followers is how they are treated within an organization. If I am always basing my moral decisions on respect for my followers, it seems evident that positive, ethical choices will be made in almost every situation I face.

Situational Leadership should be the flagship class for individuals seeking to become leaders. Because of the human dynamic at play in any relationship, leaders must be able to adapt and "...read the situation and modify [their] style to match the predicament [they] are in" (Chapman, 2018, p. 17). Humans cannot be robots who always act the same way, whether that person is a leader or follower. "[Situational leadership] offers the benefits of combined strategies that apply consideration to individual and environmental needs" (Walls, 2019, p. 31). Human nature requires that leaders be directive during some situations and supportive in others because no two people or situations can be treated the same.

According to Northouse (2014), "Directive behaviors clarify, often with one-way communication, what is to be done, how it is to be done, and who is responsible for doing it" (p. 96). As a teacher/leader in my classroom, the most consistent time I commit to this style of leadership behavior is when I am engaging students as a large group. When I address an entire class or, on a larger scale, a whole grade level of the school, there is little room for any other type of communication. At that point, my job is to relay a message to my followers and get them on board to follow directions. Utilizing any other delivery method would harm my desired outcome because of the environment. In those situations, I am one person directing sometimes hundreds of students to accomplish a task. Commanding their attention, providing clear instructions, and indicating the expectations must be done directly if our collective goal is to be achieved.

Virtually opposite of a directive approach is a supportive approach, defined by Northouse (2014) as involving "...two-way communication and responses that show social and emotional support to others" (p. 96). I often initiate this type of leadership with small groups of students, often in one-on-one situations. If I am communicating with students in this type of environment, the desired outcome is likely of a personal nature. Sometimes, students may need further clarification from the extensive group discussion, need support because of a unique problem, or have done something positive that needs to be acknowledged privately.

Leaders who utilize a situational style must know their followers to be effective. "Situational leadership requires the person leading to be flexible and modify their behaviour to suit individuality rather than using a single approach" (Wells, 2019, p. 33). As a leader in my classroom, I float between styles depending on the students with whom I am working. In a class I am teaching currently, there are a variety of personalities. I have one student on whom I must stay and constantly remind to get back on task very assertively. Because I know him, I know this is how I can help him be successful. However, I have a student who would never respond well to the same directive style in the same class. She requires more coddling and less forceful language. If I never took the time to get to know those students as individuals, it would be easy to make mistakes in my handling of situations with them. The ultimate goal of the class is for students to learn and earn credit. To make this happen, I vary my style to match what my followers need.

As with all leadership styles, there are even more breakdowns of the situational approach and its associated behaviors. The key is the high number of options a leader can integrate in a given scenario. Within the situational approach, the leader's behaviors can be manipulated to ensure followers reach the desired result successfully. Depending on the situation, I can direct, achieve, listen, share, and coach.

When the leader of an organization is not a savior but acts as a coach trying to assist everyone in the organization to become the best version of themselves, adaptive leadership is utilized. Dyle (2017) describes an adaptive leadership style as necessary because of the increasing international competition where leaders must teach the organization members how to navigate the ever-changing workplace successfully (p. 18). Critical to successfully implementing an adaptive leadership style is recognizing the followers as the primary focus, not the leader. The leader is the individual who is required to acknowledge what the followers need to be successful and then put it in place in the organization.

What is practical about the adaptive approach to leadership is the acknowledgment that things are constantly changing, and no person can recognize everything happening inside an organization. To overcome this, leaders "...should listen selectively to balance the collective views of the group" (Doyle, 2017, p. 20). In large organizations, it is next to impossible to hear the personal perspective of every group member. Therefore, adaptive leaders must talk to a cross-section of people willing to share the truth about how followers are feeling or what they notice going on in the organization. Through the conversations leaders have with followers, teachable moments are recognized to "...help people change and adjust to new situations" (Northouse, 2014, p. 290). These are often tough conversations about intense topics that need to be addressed but are often overlooked or unrecognized.

Dudley (2010) described in his TED Talk instances of "lollipop moments" where a leader does not even know they are a leader, and I look at these moments as a form of adaptive leadership. Often, all it takes to lead is to know what is going on and see what followers need. Northouse's (2014) idea of "Getting on the Balcony" (p. 262) places a leader in a position to effect change where it matters because they are taking the time to witness rather than be told what is happening in a somewhat informal ('lollipop') manner. This is when a leader acts adaptively because the follower's true importance is shown when the leader legitimately takes the time to be in the followers' shoes.

Authentic Leadership revolves around leaders' ability to be self-aware, accurate, and honest

(Northouse, 2014, p. 193). Authentic leaders know who they are and never try to be something they are not. People today are leery about their surroundings because of how much has gone on in the world around them; therefore, "...they long for bona fide leadership they can trust and for leaders who are honest and good people" (Northouse, 2014, p. 193). No matter the situation, a leader must be unafraid to be up-front, honest, and sincere with the organization.

One key to being an authentic leader is to provide expectations to followers on the front end. A genuine leader sets the tone for how they expect the organization's members to behave so they can go forth confidently to meet those expectations without being micromanaged. This gives leaders the time to do what they are supposed to: lead while providing followers with the autonomy to gain confidence, be creative, and take calculated risks without fear of being watched all the time.

Having been a follower in an organization where micromanagement is the norm, I can appreciate the necessity of being a leader who trusts my followers. As a follower, I have tried to prove to my leader that I can be authorized to make quality, informed decisions; however, I have never been able to act on my own. This causes my self-confidence to diminish because it feels like I am not competent enough to be given the autonomy to complete the task independently. I have found that this hinders my creativity in many ways, hurting the product I have been asked to create.

I have witnessed the power of providing followers with authentic leadership inside my Yearbook classroom. At the onset of the class, I was clear about my expectations for the quality of work, the time required to edit the project, and the overall positive attitude about the often tedious process. Then, I let go and let them 'be' who they are regarding their approach to completing their portion of the project. As followers, they start a bit timid and nervous about doing something wrong, and I have to coach them into trusting themselves and not asking if every move they make is perfect. A few weeks into the class, they become naturally invested in their portion of the project and how they can help other class members complete their assigned sections.

The best part of using an authentic leadership approach is the honesty required in using it. Because of this honesty, times exist when the leader learns from the follower and is not afraid to admit when a follower is more knowledgeable about something than the leader. The authentic leader does not lose control of an organization by admitting a deficiency; instead, more respect is garnered from the followers. "Authentic leaders are always aware of their strengths and weaknesses and try to overcome these shortcomings" (Saeed & Ali, 2019, p. 171). Providing my Yearbook students with the autonomy to take risks and try out ideas has allowed me to learn from them. I have learned more from my students about innovative ways to create layouts and how to use technology than any class I could ever take. Even better is their pride when they can show me and their classmates what they can accomplish. This puts other followers in a position to be willing to take a risk and put themselves out there because they know as a leader, I welcome their ideas and encourage them to become better by giving them the space necessary to do so.

Leadership is multifaceted; therefore, leaders should be malleable according to what is needed by the most influential people in an organization: the followers. Choosing a singular approach to leadership without consideration of ethics, what an organization needs, what the followers within the organization require, and the situation at hand is a dangerous way to lead. As a leader, I aspire to be able to incorporate a variety of strategies specific to whatever is happening to best serve my followers in whatever situation we find ourselves in because "...there is never a one size fits all approach to leadership" (Chapman, 2019, p. 16). I never want to think I am more important than the people I surround myself with. There is merit in the hierarchical structure because accountability is necessary; however, a leader should never make followers feel like they are less than others. Finally, I want to always be respectful and authentic with both my followers and me so that everyone knows where they stand and does not feel left in the dark. Finally, While I intend to utilize the situational and adaptive approaches to leadership quite a bit, I believe that if required to choose one, my final leadership destination will be as an authentic leader who allows followers to have a voice I am willing to listen to help them and our organization be successful.

Again, pause for a moment and reflect on Dr. Scott's applications of leadership theory. What stood out and resonated with you? What points do you agree with? What points do you disagree with? What statements could use further investigation for your leadership development?

REFLECT HERE...

THE IMPORTANCE OF
LEADERSHIP PRESENCE

Though similarities and differences exist in the leadership theories, categories, and applications described above through the insights of Dr. Creech and Dr. Scott, two commonalities exist: the importance of presence and influence. First, let us work through presence. A leader's presence may be at one extreme of micromanagement and overbearing or the other extreme of minimal presence, in name or title only. It may be a healthy, balanced amount of presence. Regardless of how much, how little, or just right, a leader's presence does exist and influences.

From 2020 to 2022, I worked with the now Dr. Karen Stewart, another of my former doctoral students. I had the privilege of jump-starting her considerations and writing process to help her throughout her dissertation journey. Her phenomenological study was *Executive Presence: African American Female Executives' Leadership Experiences During America's Racial Awakening and COVID-19.* Dr. Stewart aspired to understand the unique experiences of African American female executives in business leadership positions and assessed the intersectionality of race, gender, and class based on Kimberlé Crenshaw's work, initially established in 1989. However, the essential foundation of her work was presence, with a specific focus on executive presence, which is defined in various ways. Stewart (2022) wrote that:

> Executive presence is a term used by business executives to describe leadership excellence which connects others via the intelligence of the heart. It incorporates a leader's skills to demonstrate maturity, awareness, self-confidence, capability to command unpredictable situations, and decision-making while maintaining an assuring, supporting tone with executive peers (Beeson, 2012). Suzanne Bates, CEO of Bates Communication, and author of All the Leader You Can Be: The Science of Achieving Extraordinary Executive Presence, described it as "the ability of the leader to engage, align, inspire, and move people to act" (Heimann, 2020, p. 58).

> Stewart's research explored the lived experiences of eleven African American female executives during the pandemic and racial awakening. During each African American female executive's interview were given two definitions of Executive Presence. The first definition of Executive Presence was "the ability of the leader to engage, align, inspire, and move people to act" (Heimann, 2020, p. 59). The second definition describes Executive Presence as incorporating a leader's skills to demonstrate maturity, awareness, self-confidence, capability to command unpredictable situations, and decision-making while maintaining an assuring, supporting tone with executive peers. After obtaining both definitions, each leader was asked to rate their self-assessed score using a scale

from 1 to 10 (one is low, ten is highest). The eleven African American female executives rated themselves with a mean of eight. Most were confident despite nine African American female executives indicating they were not valued, treated, and acknowledged in the organization within the past two years. Three participants left their organization due to a lack of equitable treatment in the past two years. They prioritized making a difference for others. When the researcher shared data from the literature review, which indicated Executive Presence is biased against women and diverse leaders, none were surprised. They commented on inequities commonly used in organizations to accurately identify and assess diverse talent.

As cited by Heimann, Heppner & Wang's (2015) study designates attributes that can be measured and enhanced with intention like "emotional intelligence, authenticity, credibility, integrity, as well as communication and interactivity as the five measurable qualities that define Executive Presence (Heimann, 2020, p. 60). Heppner asserts seven attributes of leadership intelligence define executive presence: "physical intelligence, emotional intelligence, heart intelligence, communication intelligence, pragmatic intelligence, neuroscience intelligence, and consciousness intelligence" (Heimann, 2020, p. 61). Executive Presence is a key attribute.

As cited in Heimann, (2020) Bates, CEO of Bates Communication, describes Executive Presence as "the ability of the leader to engage, align, inspire, and move people to act" (Heimann, 2020, p. 59). Additional research articulates descriptors "Three qualities encompass Executive Presence: character, substance, and style (Heppner & Wang, 2015, p. 17). Heppner further states Executive Presence describes "someone who, by virtue of their effect he or she has on an audience, exerts influence beyond that conferred by formal authority" (Heppner & Wang, 2015, p. 1). Ehrlich (2011) indicates, "Presence is not some innate quality that you either have or do not. It is a set of learned behaviors that enable you to command attention. And when you are fully present, it inspires others" (p. 1). Figure 11 below offers an assessment of Executive Presence authenticity which contributes to varying factors for consideration of behaviors.

Figure 1

Inventory Diagnostic for Assessing Components of Authenticity for Executive Presence

Psychological Capital			Positive Moral Perspective			Self- Awareness/ Self- Regulation		
Does the employee effectively project confidence?	Yes	No	Does the employee exclusively act in a moral manner?	Yes	No	Does the employee possess an awareness of his or her unique talents, strengths, and sense of purpose?	Yes	No
Is the employee consistently optimistic?	Yes	No	Does the employee have a transparent and ethical decision making process?	Yes	No	Does the employee have a basic and fundamental awareness of one's knowledge, experience, and capabilities?	Yes	No
Is the employee hopeful that situations will have positive outcomes?	Yes	No	Is the employee capable of addressing ethical issues in a courageous and resilient manner?	Yes	No	Is the employee able to demonstrate an understanding of his or her identity, emotions, and motives/goals?	Yes	No
Does the employee show resiliency when faced with challenges?	Yes	No	Does the employee demonstrate an ability to further develop moral capacity, efficacy, courage, and resiliency?	Yes	No	Can the employee show self-control/restraint by (a) setting internal standards, (b) assessing discrepancies between these standards and actual or expected outcomes, and (c) identifying intended actions for reconciling these discrepancies?	Yes	No
Leadership Processes/Behaviors			**Veritable and Sustained Performance Beyond Expectations**			**Total Yes Count** _____		
Does the employee lead by example?	Yes	No	Does the employee use ethical values to attained sustained performance?	Yes	No	**Total No Count** _____		
Does the employee demonstrate consistency between their words and actions?	Yes	No	Does the employee demonstrate an understanding of how the organization is fundamentally run?	Yes	No	**Yes/No Ratio** _____		
Does the employee engage in positive social exchanges with others?	Yes	No	Is the employee consistently delivering performance above what is expected?	Yes	No	**Notes:**		
Can the employee leverage positive emotions to foster the emotional and cognitive development of other organizational members?	Yes	No	Does the employee demonstrate persistent growth over a period of time?	Yes	No			

Note. From Heppner, S., and Wang, T. (April 1, 2015). *What are the measurable qualities that define Executive Presence and how can we use it to tangibly assess leaders?* Cornell University Library Digital Collections. https://hdl.handle.net/1813/74513

Heppner and Wang (2015) illustrated examples using pseudonym names: Frank, Alice, and Lydia. As executives considered Frank, who was a collaborative, accomplished leader was considered a successor due to his accomplishments and collaborative nature, yet his attire was rumpled (Beeson, 2012). While presenting, he was viewed as professional but wordy; he did not step in when executives were in intense debates and deferred to the executive team's leadership often. Frank was knowledgeable and well-prepared but not capable of leading business with customers. Alice was highly capable with each project she led, yet she was not selected for senior-level advancement due to her disorganization.

Beeson (2012) concluded the pseudonym example Lydia, could be missed in a room with other leaders until dialogue began then she was respected by everyone and ready for challenges. Lydia questioned others and firmly "stood her ground in a non-confrontational way" (Beeson, 2012, p. 3) Lydia has demonstrated the justification as "the top successor and prepared for the organization's General Counsel role" (Beeson, 2012, p. 3). Lydia demonstrated Executive Presence by knowing when to speak up, step back, and use humor. She instinctively challenged when an option was too risky for the organization. Lydia's mastery, command, and emotional intelligence illustrated her mastery of Executive Presence.

Judgment, listening skills, and self-control influence the assessment of your Executive Presence (Beeson, 2012). Presentation skills greatly influence "your ability to stand and deliver to an executive group or large audience is frequently viewed as an indicator of your ability to handle pressure" (Beeson, 2012, p. 4).

Executive Presence is inconsistently defined, used incongruously, and influences many C-suite promotions (Beeson, 2012). A lack of Executive Presence contributes to less organizational senior leadership exposure and relationships.

Senior leaders in large organizations may not know who is working on their team due to the size and complex infrastructure required for talent to accomplish tasks (Coleman, 2010). They may become aware of talent based on recent wins or successes without actual knowledge of the person's skills and capability to achieve goals:

First, few senior executives (except those in very small organizations) will know everyone in their areas of responsibility. Second, unless the definition of high potential is made quite clear, senior executives are likely to respond to a request for names based on their perceptions. Perceptions about individuals can be overly colored by recent events (recency bias), extremely bad incidents (the horn effect), or extremely good incidents (the halo effect). Indeed, perceptions can lead to personal favoritism, discrimination, or pigeon-holing in which individual potential is difficult to change once assessed. (Rothwell, 2010, p. 227)

Many senior leaders mentor their successors and often provide valuable insight regarding each candidate's capability (Northouse, 2019). Some senior leaders enjoy close personal relationships with successors based on many things they share in common, leading to a "like me bias" without their awareness (Rothwell, 2010). Similar interests like sports can influence personal connectivity, yet female successors may not desire non-work activities where such bonding occurs (Coleman, 2010). Comfort, familiarity, and commonality can frequently be mistaken for potential when senior leaders offer highly visible projects and critical assignments based on affiliation and exposure (Coleman, 2010).

Again, pause for a moment and reflect on Dr. Stewart's applications of leadership theory. What stood out and resonated with you? What points do you agree with? What points do you disagree with? What statements could use further investigation for your leadership development?

REFLECT HERE...

LEADERSHIP INFLUENCE AND SERVANT LEADERSHIP

Influence. Impact. Imprint. These are powerful words. They are loaded words too. Scripture is unequivocal on our ability to influence others positively or negatively. These principles are explored in various places throughout this book, as how we impact and leave an imprint on their lives. However, before we proceed to the next chapter, as we consider the characteristics of leadership, take some time to reflect on who has influenced you in your life – a parent, a sibling, a friend, a neighbor, a pastor, a coworker, a boss. How have these individuals influenced and left their mark on you?

REFLECT HERE...

Next, likely, the individuals who came to mind in the previous paragraph and your reflection were not always positive. One of the prevailing theories of leadership is servant leadership. This leadership style will be explored further when considering the Biblical Principles of Leadership in Chapter 4 and then when studying the leadership of The Master Leader in Chapter 8. So, for now, a more cursory look is provided on servant leadership.

Michael (2024a) stated, "Servant leadership is a leadership philosophy where the leader's main purpose is to serve their followers. The term was first brought to the public eye by Robert Greenleaf in his 1973 essay The Servant as Leader and has since inspired many to trade in the old concept of leadership as a top-down model to be more focused on the needs and wants of the followers." Leadership is shared and democratic, allowing for buy-in from followers and coworkers. The approach places the needs of others first, and in a corporate, organizational sense, it addresses how I can help the individuals working under me succeed.

To provide a sense of how servant leadership works and what it looks like in a contemporary company or organization, consider the following quotes, organized by last name, as collected by Michael (2024b).

- "The servant leader believes that 'my success is your success.'" – Anonymous
- "It's not about trying to find something to help you be a more effective leader. It's about trying to be a better person. The other will follow." – James A. Autry
- "Servant leadership is all about making the goals clear and then rolling your sleeves up and doing whatever it takes to help people win. In that situation, they don't work for you; you work for them." – Ken Blanchard
- "Serving people means growing their capacity and implies that everyone can contribute." – Juana Bordas
- "The servant-leader is servant first. It begins with the natural feeling that one wants to serve, to serve first. Then conscious choice brings one to aspire to lead." – Robert K. Greenleaf
- "People do not care how much you know until they know how much you care." – John C. Maxwell
- "The goal of many leaders is to get people to think more highly of the leader. The goal of a great leader is to help people to think more highly of themselves." – J. Carla Northcutt
- "Leaders don't create more followers; they create more leaders." – Tom Peters
- "A leader is best when people barely know he exists, when his work is done, his aim fulfilled, they will say: we did it ourselves." – Lao Tzu

- "We must be silent before we can listen. We must listen before we can learn. We must learn before we can prepare. We must prepare before we can serve. We must serve before we can lead." – William Arthur Ward
- "If you want to lift yourself up, lift up someone else." – Booker Washington
- "I'll lift you and you'll lift me and we'll both ascend together." – John Greenleaf Whittier
- "The ear of the leader must ring with the voices of the people." – Woodrow Wilson

Wow, the quotes above show a lot related to servant leadership. Imagine the level of influence and impact that can flow out of a leader who exhibits these qualities. As we close out this chapter and transition to a deeper dive into leadership characteristics, I encourage you to go back and re-read this list of quotes compiled by Michael (2024b). Take some time to mark them up, process their wisdom, and reflect in the section below.

REFLECT HERE ON CHAPTER THOUGHTS, REACTIONS, RESPONSES, ACTION ITEMS...

CHAPTER THREE

KEY LEADERSHIP CHARACTERISTICS AND FOLLOWERSHIP

This chapter explores the characteristics of leadership and what describes a good leader versus a bad one; additionally, followership is explored. Another way to consider these characteristics is to ask the question, what is an effective versus ineffective leader? Books, articles, blogs, podcasts, and more abound associated with this topic. Conduct a simple Google or Amazon search, and the matches for this topic are endless. While the previous chapter explored prominent leadership theories, this chapter focuses more on the characteristics and what the "experts" tell us about good, effective leadership.

Again, with my experience of teaching leadership courses in higher education, both at the master's level and at the doctoral level, the question of what makes a good, effective leader as opposed to a bad, ineffective leader is always a solid starting point when considering characteristics. Asking this question to ourselves and discussing it with others in a classroom setting, in the break room, with a friend or colleague, or simply mulling it about in our minds can generate a lot of potential answers. Making a list of these characteristics can be a great exercise, and in doing so, when discussed with others, it can be a powerful tool for consideration.

Additionally, discussing these characteristics can be productive; sadly, the opposite is likely to be accurate, too, as some of us have been devastated and hurt by those in leadership positions over us. It is assumed that specific people will come to mind as we consider characteristics, whether good and effective or bad and ineffective. As hard as it may be, for this chapter's consideration, try your best to focus on the characteristics exhibited by the leader versus the person, as I want to remind you again of the goal of this book. It is not a revenge tour. Instead, this book has collected principles and stories of what not to do to be an effective, good leader. It draws upon history, Scripture, and personal experience, providing insights into what to avoid or not do to be a great leader.

Before you continue reading this chapter, I encourage you, either in your mind or in the section below, to conduct a brainstorming session related to the two critical questions of this chapter.

- What makes a good, effective leader?
- What makes a bad, ineffective leader?

REFLECT HERE...

When I have posed this question to my graduate-level students over the years, it has been fascinating to hear what they say. While many characteristics are consistent from one group to the next, some outlier responses sometimes exist. Embedded with each person's responses and list of characteristics is always a few stories, encounters, or seasons of experience.

LEADERSHIP SUCCINCTLY DEFINED

Northouse (2019) wrote that defining leadership is an exceedingly difficult endeavor. He noted that leadership "is much like democracy, love, and peace. Although we intuitively know what we mean by such words, the words can have different meanings for different people." Generational, historical, cultural, and contextual factors influence the meaning and understanding of the concept of leadership. The *Oxford Dictionary* defines leadership as "the action of leading a group of people or an organization." McKinsey et al. (2022) said that leadership "is a set of behaviors used to help people align their collective direction, to execute strategic plans, and to continually renew an organization." W.C.H. Prentice (2004) wrote in the *Harvard Leadership Review*, "Leadership is an interaction among people. It requires followers with particular traits and particular skills and a leader who knows how to use them."

Finally, after considering the definitions offered by respected business thinkers such as Peter Drucker, Warren Bennis, Bill Gates, and John Maxwell, Kruse (2013), writing for *Forbes,* created this definition: "Leadership is a process of social influence, which maximizes the efforts of others, towards the achievement of a goal." Then Kruse explained what was meant by the critical elements of his definition. He wrote:

- "Leadership stems from social influence, not authority or power.
- Leadership requires others, and that implies they don't need to be 'direct reports.'
- No mention of personality traits, attributes, or even a title; there are many styles, and many paths, to effective leadership.
- It includes a goal, not influence with no intended outcome."

As J.C. Rost (1991) stated, "After decades of dissonance, leadership scholars agree on one thing: They can't come up with a common definition for leadership. Because of such factors as growing global influences and generational differences, leadership will continue to have different meanings for different people. The bottom line is that leadership is a complex concept for which a determined definition may long be in flux."

Nevertheless, amidst the difficulties of succinctly and accurately defining the concept and reality of leadership, take a moment to pause, reflect, and create your definition of leadership. Then, continue to the next section of this chapter, which explores this topic with some qualifiers: good, effective as opposed to bad, and ineffective.

REFLECT HERE...

GOOD, EFFECTIVE LEADERSHIP

Good. Effective. What do these words mean in general? What do they mean in the context of leadership? What do (or should) they look like in a company or organization? If you conduct an Internet search, you will likely be overwhelmed with lists of characteristics and traits that describe a good, effective leader. Much of what you see will probably connect to the suggested exercise earlier in this chapter. But now let us briefly consider how some contemporary research experts have included on their lists. Here are a few of them.

The Center for Creative Leadership's 10 Essential Leadership Traits (2023):

1. Integrity
2. Delegation
3. Communication
4. Self-Awareness
5. Gratitude
6. Learning Agility
7. Influence
8. Empathy
9. Courage
10. Respect

Forbes' 8 Essential Qualities That Define Great Leadership (Fries, 2018)

1. Sincere Enthusiasm
2. Integrity
3. Great Communication Skills
4. Loyalty

5. Decisiveness
6. Managerial Competence
7. Empowerment
8. Charisma

Tony Robbins' Elevate Your Impact: 10 Leadership Qualities of Remarkable Leaders (Robbins, 2024)

1. Extraordinary Hunger
2. Compelling Vision
3. Effective and Influential Communication
4. Brilliant Strategist
5. Authentic and Congruent
6. Absolute Certainty
7. Committed Yet Flexible
8. Courage and Faith
9. Ability to Connect and Break Patterns
10. Unreasonable Expectations and Standards

Sarmad Hasan's Top 15 Leadership Qualities That Make Good Leaders (2024)

1. Honesty and integrity
2. Confidence
3. Inspire Others
4. Commitment and Passion
5. Good Communicator
6. Decision Making Capabilities
7. Accountability
8. Delegation and Empowerment
9. Creativity and Innovation
10. Empathy
11. Resilience

12. Emotional Intelligence
13. Humility
14. Transparency
15. Vision and Purpose

John Maxwell's 4Cs of Leadership and then his 21 Indispensable Qualities of a Leader (31West, 2023; Maxwell, 2020)

- Competence, Candor, Connect, Character

1. Character: Be a Piece of the Rock
2. Charisma: The First Impression Can Steal the Deal
3. Commitment: It Separates Doers from Dreamers
4. Communication: Without It, You Travel Alone
5. Competence: If You Build It, They Will Come
6. Courage: One Person with Courage Is a Majority
7. Discernment: Put an End to Unsolved Mysteries
8. Focus: The Sharper It Is, the Sharper You Are
9. Generosity: Your Candle Loses Nothing When It Lights Another
10. Initiative: You Won't Leave Home Without It
11. Listening: To Connect with Their Hearts, Use Your Ears
12. Passion: Take This Life and Love It
13. Positive Attitude: If You Believe You Can, You Can
14. Problem-Solving: You Can't Let Your Problems Be a Problem
15. Relationships: If You Get Along, They'll Go Along
16. Responsibility: If You Won't Carry the Ball, You Can't Lead the Team
17. Security: Competence Never Compensates for Insecurity

18. Self-Discipline: The First Person You Lead Is You
19. Servanthood: To Get Ahead, Put Others First
20. Teachability: To Keep Leading, Keep Learning
21. Vision: You Can Seize Only What You Can See

Before you continue, I encourage you to go back and reread those contemporary experts' lists. Slow down. Take a pause. Be reflective as you ponder these questions:

- How do the experts' lists compare and contrast your personal list?
- Do the experts' characteristics describe leaders you have worked for in the past? The present?
- Which characteristics from the experts' lists are easily identifiable?
- Which characteristics do you long to see?

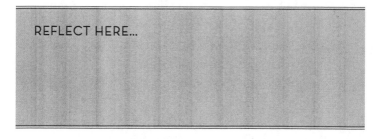

REFLECT HERE...

Now, do some self-reflection. Do these characteristics describe you from your lists and the experts' lists? Do you think that others would agree or disagree with your self-assessment? Could you be so bold as to put the book down to talk with a trusted friend or colleague to see what they think about your self-assessment?

REFLECT HERE...

You have heard from a few research experts. Now consider what some "real folks" said when posed with the following prompt – "Leadership is...." Thanks to the dear friend and former doctoral student who posed this question and helped gather responses to include below. Also, thank you to those who contributed to this opportunity to respond to this prompt.

Leadership is...

- Taking care of your people.
- A commitment to people and the task at hand.
- Stepping back so others can step forward and magically, at the same time, do the work WITH them.
- Being present, accountable, and not taking advantage of one's position/authority.
- Collective and involves guiding and encouraging others.
- Taking all the blame yourself and giving all the credit to others.
- Reflective, constantly taking the time to grow, move forward, and improve.
- Helping others grow and building them up to see their potential.

- Building up your team so nobody can tell who the leader is.
- Being humble!
- Empowering your people to be decision-makers and "happen" makers.
- Setting the tone, climate, and expectations for your organization.
- Guiding individuals and groups in your organization to grow and thrive.
- The modeling of making mistakes, falling forward, and empowering those around you to do the same.
- Never make the work about you but for your organization, people, and customers.
- Being willing to say, "I was wrong. I made a mistake. I am sorry. We will correct this and do better going forward."
- Empower your people to exemplify their strengths and grow in their weaknesses for the betterment and success of the whole team.
- Dependability, accountability, advocacy, and humility.
- Is being an example, leading supportively, and creating a climate allowing individual talents to develop the best team possible to do the job.
- It is listening and knowing when to step in and when to step back. It involves trusting the team you have built.
- Self-awareness brings and promotes authenticity and is concerned with building others up and a team.
- Listening, being positive, setting a positive tone, and leading by example.

- Being real, respectful, working together, listening, and being an active part of a team.
- Involves being effective and possessing a positive attitude, encouraging others, embracing failure, exhibiting a sense of humor, and listening carefully to others.
- Knows how and when to delegate, is growth-oriented, and demonstrates responsibility and perseverance.
- The process of influencing people by providing purpose, direction, and motivation while improving the organization.
- Involves passion and taking steps to inspire, problem solve, move to action, and exercise discipline, consistency, and impartiality.
- Say "good morning" to all, regardless of their status or position in the organization, and treat everyone with respect and impartiality.
- Being humble enough to admit when you are wrong.
- Caring about people over tasks and giving everyone a seat at the table to contribute.
- Putting what is best for the group/mission over personal gain and recognition – we over me.
- Being present and building a relationship with those who fall under you.
- Believing in your team and truly recognizing the value in them.
- Leading by example and not just distributing information. It models your expectations!
- Leadership is HARD. And, unless you have been in that position, you likely have no clue as to all it entails. Period. So, give others the benefit of the doubt, as you never know the struggles that they are

going through, especially if you do not genuinely care or ask.

- Is honest, even if uncomfortable; otherwise, there is no trust. Then, it is holding people accountable for their mistakes while encouraging learning and praising them when they do well.

Wow. What a list. Again, before you continue to the next section of this chapter, I strongly encourage you to go back and take some time to look at the responses given by "real folks."

Then, consider taking the time to work through these questions. Do these characteristics describe leaders you have worked for in the past? The present? What characteristics are easily identifiable? Which characteristics do you long to see? Now, do some self-reflection. Do these characteristics describe you? Would others agree or disagree with your self-assessment? As suggested before, with the experts' lists, could you do the same: be bold and put the book down to talk with a trusted friend or colleague to see what they think about your self-assessment?

REFLECT HERE...

Warning, dear reader. Next, we move into the uncomfortable, the hard, and the downright difficult. In doing so, remember the goal of this book. What can be learned? How can situations and people be redeemed? How can leaders, and more on a personal level, and how can you grow and develop as a leader? Here we go.

BAD, INEFFECTIVE LEADERSHIP

A great friend recently said, "Being a good, effective leader is really hard. It takes intentionality. When not properly checked, the same level of intentionality can also lead to bad, ineffective leadership." As we considered earlier in this chapter, let us first examine what some contemporary experts say. According to Hannah Price (2019), describing a bad, ineffective leader can be summed up with six "lack" statements:

1. Lack of presence
2. Lack of directions
3. Lack of transparency
4. Lack of authority
5. Lack of listening skills
6. Lack of faith

Another perspective of bad, ineffective leadership comes from Hyatt-Fennell (2023), an industry leader in executive-level leadership searches, training, and coaching. Their brief article, *Top Traits of a Horrible Leader*, listed three characteristics provided below. Still, in this article, they made a powerful statement using research found in the work of Development Dimensions International's (DDI) *Frontline Leader Project* (Almes, 2019). The famous adage "people don't quit a job, they quit a boss" was affirmed by their research, which found the following about poor leaders: a) 57 percent of employees have left a job because of their boss(es), and b) 32 percent have seriously considered leaving because of their boss(es). The percentage left is astounding. Only 11 percent of employees were satisfied and content with staying at their job due to good, effective boss(es). Yikes!

Hyatt-Fennell (2023) stated, "The biggest indicator of a team's success is their leader. Employees will stay the course of a difficult project under the direction of a quality leader. Conversely, even routine operations become dysfunctional drudgery under a poor manager."

- Micromanagement
- Unclear expectations
- Narcissism

While Price's (2019) and Hyatt-Fennell's (2023) lists were more characteristic-driven, John Maxwell (2019) wrote in his book *How to Lead When Your Boss Won't (Or Can't)* that one fundamental reality will occur in an organization as a result of bad, ineffective leadership. This reality is drift, and the following will inevitably arise due to drift.

- Decisions are delayed.
- Agendas are multiplied.
- Conflicts are extended.
- Morale becomes low.
- Production is reduced.
- Success is difficult.
- The vision of the organization suffers.

Before we continue to consider the characteristics, challenges, and likely results of poor leadership, take some time to reflect on Price's (2019) "lack" statements and Maxwell's (2019) emphasis on drift and the inevitable negative results that will follow. Again, Maxwell writes in the book mentioned above that "if you've ever been frustrated by a boss who wouldn't [effectively] lead, you're not alone... You don't need to be the boss or have a great boss to be successful." (back cover)

REFLECT HERE...

You have heard again from a couple of research experts, and as we did before, let us consider again what some "real folks" had to say when posed with the following prompt – "Poor, ineffective leadership is..."

Thank you to those who contributed to this opportunity when I posted this prompt for reflection and response. And yes, in full disclosure, when given the exact scope of opportunity and time to respond to the prompts, many responses below were shorter, and the overall number of responses was more significant.

Poor, ineffective leadership is...

- The downfall of potential greatness.
- Stifling and frustrating.
- When one does not listen to or value the opinion of those they lead.

- Usually a matter of self-interest, not lack of competence. It is easy to be or become competent; leading in the interests of those shown is challenging.
- Leads to systemic organizational problems.
- Self-reliance.
- Directly related to the slow or stunted growth within an organization.
- Begins with being a poor example yourself, e.g., exhibiting few qualities you expect to see in a strong, wise leader.
- Toxic.
- A lack of shepherding those in your "flock" with integrity, upright heart, and a skillful hand. (Psalm 78:72)
- The critical component in apathetic performance.
- A lack of trust in your team by micromanaging them and not allowing their ideas or input. Instead, have a propensity to listen and say YES to your team as much as possible.
- Afraid to entertain questions and often forbids them.
- Creates chaos because no cohesive model exists for making plans or resolving issues.
- Detrimental to productivity.
- Breeds discontent among co-workers.
- The beginning of a slow train wreck.
- Completely draining to those being "led."
- Hypocritical.
- Is not leadership...a leader is a person who takes the initiative to influence a group of people towards a common purpose. So, if they are not doing that, they are not leading. They are just in the way.

- Apparent to clients/customers, etc., when they notice poor customer service, uninformed staff, the disorderly appearance of the facility, etc.
- Only lead with those with whom you agree.
- Avoiding confrontation.
- Demoralizing.
- Lacks clear and open communication. It is a recipe for low morale and discontent among employees. It is an inevitable spiral down.
- Uninspiring and toxic. It establishes a culture of having to and not wanting to (e.g., I have to do this task vs. I want to do it). It sets a bad example for future potential leaders and can lead to continuing the same culture.
- Not leadership at all.
- Uninspiring.
- Detrimental to the culture and effectiveness of any organization.
- A failure for everyone involved!
- Stifling.
- Corrosive to the workplace environment.
- Leads to poor, ineffective results.
- Leads from a place of position, not a place of service.
- Do this because I said so, and I am in charge instead of letting me show you how I would like this done.
- Selfishness.
- An unfortunate reality in today's world.
- Based on feelings, not organized, indecisive, without goals, and plays favorites.
- The failure to see people as people.
- Presumptive of everyone being on the same page rather than laying out a vision and confirming that

everyone is on the same page (or at least transparent on the vision and strategies to get there)!

- Passive, aggressive, and fear-based.
- Likely often done unintentionally, or maybe it is not.
- Who starts your day with "we need to talk" too frequently, thus making you feel stressed and nervous.
- Driven by insecurities and devoid of humility.
- Creates more work for employees, lowering productivity and innovation while creating a hostile culture.
- Not listening.
- Crushing to the employees serving under that leader.
- Not collaborative and built on fear.
- Can be corrected with proper training in emotional intelligence, and they must also have an open mind and heart.
- Avoidable.
- Sadly, the norm.
- Prioritizing the institution's image and accolades over the prosperity and welfare of its people.
- Tragically, more often than not, it is the new norm.
- Evidenced by a failure to create positive and productive relationships.
- Crippling and demoralizing, breeding an atmosphere of toxicity, chaos, and uncertainty, whether intentional or not, resulting in the downfall of not only the individual but that of the institution/entity itself.

Wow. Again, what a list. Furthermore, before you continue to the next section of this chapter, I strongly encourage you to go back and take some time to look at the responses given by "real folks."

REFLECT HERE...

Then, consider taking the time to work through these questions. Do these characteristics describe leaders you have worked for in the past? The present? What characteristics are easily identifiable? Which characteristics do you long to see? Now, do some self-reflection. Do these characteristics describe you? Would others agree or disagree with your self-assessment? As suggested before, with the experts' lists, could you do the same: be bold and put the book down to talk with a trusted friend or colleague to see what they think about your self-assessment?

REFLECT HERE...

Next, we move into the critical topic of followership. As evidenced above, with experts' and real folks' assessment of good, effective, and bad, ineffective leadership, a leader's desire, ability, and action to create followership is essential. As we will explore in Chapter 4, Scripture also gives more attention to followership than leadership.

INTENTIONAL ASIDE –
AN EMPHASIS ON FOLLOWERSHIP

Another of my former doctoral students, whom I had the privilege of guiding through her dissertation journey, is Dr. Kimberly Champagne, who, in some circles, is known as a Professor of Business or Lieutenant Colonel in the United States Air Force. Her dissertation research, completed in 2023, focused on Air Force commanders' perceptions of the Master Sergeants' readiness to take on the demands of leading airmen and following their leaders. Her research investigated the use of aspects of the Leader-Member Exchange (LMX) theory between Air Force commanders and Master Sergeants regarding training and developing Master Sergeants' skills to be commensurate with their ranks.

One of the essential parts of her research and the literature surrounding leadership included followership, which is the concept of reaching a specific goal while exercising respect for authority, taking the initiative, having humility, a positive attitude, integrity, and self-discipline. Again, I thank Dr. Champagne for her permission to provide her findings and insights on the topic of followership explored below. Her dissertation's title was *Using Leader-Member Exchange Theory as a Predictor of Master Sergeants' Positive Work Outcomes*.

> When joining the Air Force, we agree to be professional, act morally and responsibly, complete tasks to the best of our ability, and have a willingness to serve our community. Effective followership is an essential element of the development of all Air Force leaders (Air Force Enlisted Force Structure Handbook, 2022; Champagne, 2023).

The failure of followership results in ineffective leadership and the subsequent collapse of an organization (Currie & Ryan, 2014). Few leaders acknowledge the power of followership when evaluating the success of their organization. However, poor work ethic and lack of followership can lead to lost opportunities, unsatisfied customers, high operational costs, compromised product and service quality, and weak competitiveness, further compromising followership (Thomas & Berg, 2020). At its extreme, weak followership and ineffective leadership are detrimental and lead to organizational confusion and poor performance.

Qualities of Good Followers. Followers must exhibit specific qualities when interacting with their leaders in an organization. First, they should have good judgment and a positive work ethic. Riggio (2020) indicated that followers are obliged to the enterprise and should thus adhere to the directives when they are ethical and when they positively impact an organization. Therefore, followers need to judge their leaders' directives to ensure that they engage in sound activities likely to foster the success of their organizations. No one disputes that a good leader must have critical judgment. The followers must also exhibit the same trait, considering that they are obligated to advise their leaders to help their leaders avoid making mistakes. McCallum (2013) explained that followers who exhibit critical, judgmental abilities have the upper hand in rising to leadership positions and replacing their leaders who retire or exit the organization. Furthermore, followers should exhibit positive work ethics by being good workers. They should show commitment, diligence, and motivation and pay attention to details. Even though the leaders are responsible for fostering a workplace culture that nurtures these qualities, the followers are obligated to ensure that they remain good workers, exhibiting these positive traits.

Followers must be competent and courageous. They can only follow and manage the tasks the leaders assign. McCallum (2013) noted that leaders can improve their followers' competence through staff development programs. Followers need basic skills and knowledge to perform tasks without relying on the direction of their leaders.

In addition to competence, followers need to show a high level of courage. In some cases, leaders can make mistakes likely to cost an organization. Followers must have the courage to confront their leaders to ensure that mistakes are not repeated to save an organization from collapse (Currie & Ryan, 2014). Courage is the foremost of the virtues upon which other values depend (Churchill, 1931). Therefore, to be a good follower takes courage, especially when pointing out and correcting mistakes committed by leaders.

Finally, followers need to be loyal and effectively manage their egos. Followership is associated with loyalty among subordinates; they are expected to support their leaders even when things are not working in their favor. According to McCallum (2013), followers with compromised loyalty are the sources of difficulties felt in an organization since they could potentially waste others' time, prevent the achievement of goals, or instigate internal employee conflicts. Therefore, followers should have a solid allegiance to their leaders and commitment to the organization's goals. However, leaders should prudently acknowledge that loyalty is not synonymous with a "Yes Man" mentality, and they should allow followers the opportunity to challenge the practices of the entity so long as such criticism is respectful. Effective loyalty is an absence of ego. Furthermore, followers should also, prudently, keep their egos under control by associating with teams and having a good sense of interpersonal skills. Followers' success relates to quality performance and goal achievement, not self-promotion and personal recognition (McCallum, 2013). Thus, the followers should work with others to promote teamwork while suppressing any feelings of competing with other team members.

The Best Types of Followers in an Organization. The success of an organization depends on the quality of the followers. The latter should contribute to the success of an organization although the role of the leaders is to foster their motivation and retention. Currie and Ryan (2014) noted that the best followers align their goals with the organization and commit their time, resources, and competence toward their attainment. Deep commitment to the success of an organization and the ability to realize individual goals distinguish the best from the worst followers. Thomas and Berg (2020) used the same argument; they indicated that the best followers pay attention to realizing the goals of an organization, while the worst followers pay attention to personal advancement, success, and gratification. Important to note is that nothing is wrong with followers having personal goals as it fosters motivation and satisfaction.

However, they should remain committed to realizing the organizational goals and follow their leaders to ensure they remain loyal, motivated, and productive in the organization (Currie & Ryan, 2014). Thus, social exchange in which the leaders appreciate the followers' loyalty is definitely needed.

Moreover, the best followers are compliant with their leaders and the organization. Compliance is exhibited through effective time management, careful monitoring of deadlines, and conscious management of resources (Currie & Ryan, 2014). Followers need to manage the resources as if they were theirs. They should minimize waste while ensuring they report all cases of theft. Compliance also implies aligning their activities with the leaders' directives. Followers must remain loyal to their leaders and organizations, ensuring their actions align with the organization's vision, values, and mission. However, McCallum (2013) expressed a contrary opinion by stating that followers should only be compliant with ethical directives, critiquing the leaders when they make mistakes likely to cost an organization. The ability to critique the leaders requires a high level of honesty and courage, at the risk of retaliation and denial of opportunities, to uphold the highest levels of morality against the status quo. Thus, compliance and loyalty should be expressed in support of the virtues of an organization to protect the entity's image.

Additionally, the best followers show advanced levels of competence. They are willing to seek opportunities to foster their skill development even when they incur costs in terms of money and time. Dynamics are present in systems, ways of doing things, and technologies; hence, the need for individuals to keep pace with the changes to foster organizational development. The best followers fear skill obsolescence and are willing to sacrifice to learn the best skills and knowledge for organizational success. Currie and Ryan (2014) noted that the best followers seek to learn more about the operations outside their areas of responsibility with the sound understanding that they may be shifted to other areas; hence, the need to stay ready with the requisite skills. The zeal to learn is also associated with personal development. Like leaders, followers need to be skilled in readiness to replace their leaders in managerial or supervisory roles should the need arise. Constant learning improves their competence, allowing them to effectively manage new positions (Currie & Ryan, 2014). Thus, the best followers pay attention to learning, and they seek to understand the operations of the organization and its subunits.

Furthermore, the best followers inspire their colleagues while acting as role models in all their actions. Even though leaders function as role models, serving as examples to their followers, this role is not only preserved for them. The responsibility of the followers, especially those who have longevity with the organization, is to be an excellent example for the newer employees to emulate (Gobble, 2017). They should exhibit a high level of dedication, fair-mindedness, and persistence in all their dealings. These characteristics can inspire the other followers to work and realize the goals of an organization. Through these traits, the best followers excel as individuals and as a group in the organization. According to Currie and Ryan (2014), good followers exercise good citizenship behavior in every aspect. They are willing to serve others, show direction, and provide the necessary support to enable their colleagues to excel beyond expectations.

Finally, the best followers interact with their leaders, contributing to the success of an organization. Interaction is an essential aspect that fosters the success of the organization. Thomas and Berg (2020) stated that interaction provides an excellent avenue for followers and leaders to share skills and knowledge needed to increase productivity. Through interaction, individuals understand an organization's values, mission, and goals and the best ways of aligning their actions with these aspects. According to Currie and Ryan (2014), interaction should be upheld but under regulation to ensure that leader-follower boundaries are not compromised. The focus of the interaction should be to build interpersonal skills like communication and conflict resolution to foster positive coexistence in the organization. Gobble (2017) noted that close interaction allows individuals to understand the values, beliefs, and perceptions of others and how they react to stimuli. As such, the followers are likely to understand the best strategies for regulating emotions to ensure that their actions do not harm the leaders and other subordinates in the organization.

Pause for a moment and reflect on Dr. Champagne's words on followership, with specifics related to the qualities of good followers and the best types of followers in an organization. What stood out and resonated with you? What points do you agree with? What points do you disagree with? What statements could use further investigation for your leadership development?

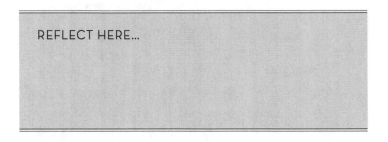

REFLECT HERE...

PROPER FOLLOWERSHIP

As we grapple with the reality of poor, ineffective leadership and its connection to followership, the many contributors to this book were asked to respond to the prompt below and take note of the insightful, valuable thoughts provided.

Proper or good followership, even if it has to happen under poor, ineffective leadership, is…

- The basis and foundation for a healthier workplace.
- Completely essential to happiness at work.
- Possible by being creative, taking initiative, and working hard. Even an ineffective leader's organization/business can shine with effective employees.
- Is a matter of professionalism. Do your job and do it well, regardless of the leader.
- The only way to survive lousy leadership. However, if it has to happen under poor, ineffective leadership, good followership can (and likely will) lead to demoralization and discouragement over time. In turn, this can lead to losing wonderful people within an organization.

The Apostle Paul, in Philippians 2, laid out what we, as good followers, should and should not do. He wrote:

> [14] Do all things *without grumbling or disputing,* [15] that you may *be blameless* and *innocent,* children of God *without blemish* in the midst of a crooked and twisted generation, among whom you *shine as lights* in the world, [16] holding fast to the word of life, so that in the day of Christ *I may be proud* that I did not run in vain or labor in vain.
> [17] Even if I am to be poured out as a drink offering upon the sacrificial offering of your faith, *I am glad and rejoice* with you all. [18] Likewise you also should be glad and rejoice with me. [emphasis added]

Do not grumble. Do not complain. Do not dispute or be argumentative. Be blameless and innocent. Look different. Shine as a light. Hold fast to who God is. Put yourself in a position to be proud of who you are and what you do. Be glad. Rejoice.

What a problematic list! I know what some or all of you are thinking. When Paul wrote this letter to the Philippians, he was not serious, right? Did he ever work for my boss? Did he ever work for my company? Indeed not, correct? The complicated answer is yes, Paul did mean what he wrote. Good followership, even with bad, ineffective leadership, looks like what he wrote to the Philippians. It is not optional. Good followership can make a positive impact, and even if it does not yield positive change in leadership within a company, it can help us grow and develop as a leader.

CHAPTER WRAP UP

As we conclude this chapter, take note of some encouragement from James. In the opening section of his letter, he reminds us to remember that troubles and tests assist us with endurance and maturity in our faith journey. He wrote the following in James 1:2-4:

> [2] *Count it all joy*, my brothers, when you meet trials of various kinds, [3] for you know that *the testing of your faith produces steadfastness.* [4] And let steadfastness have its full effect, that you may be *perfect and complete, lacking in nothing.* [emphasis added]

Steadfastness, perfect, complete, lacking in nothing. Amidst bad, poor, ineffective, toxic leadership experiences, may God use these people to mold us into men and women who fit the description provided by James, and as we navigate bad, ineffective leadership experiences, may we do what James goes on to say in James 1:5. "If any of you lacks wisdom, let him ask God, who gives generously to all without reproach, and it will be given him."

REFLECT HERE ON CHAPTER THOUGHTS, REACTIONS, RESPONSES, ACTION ITEMS...

CHAPTER FOUR

BIBLICAL PRINCIPLES OF LEADERSHIP

OCCURRENCES IN SCRIPTURE

Leadership principles abound in Scripture, and many references exist directly and indirectly from Genesis to Revelation. This chapter focuses on occurrences and principles of leadership, followers, and servants from the Bible, and then Chapter 8 gives specific, intentional attention to The Master Leader, Jesus. I encourage you to take your time working through this chapter, especially when you get to the section containing specific passages of Scripture.

Depending on the version or translation of the Bible you consult, the words "leadership," "leader," and "lead" may be minimally used. For instance, in the King James Version (KJV), the word "leadership" does not appear. Also, in the KJV, "leader" appears only three times – in 1 Chronicles 12:27, 1 Chronicles 13:1, and Isaiah 55:4. Then, all other forms of the word "lead" appear 81 times (Ritenbaugh, 2024).

In comparison, in the New International Version (NIV), leadership is only found four times – in Numbers 27:18,

Numbers 33:1, Psalm 109:8, and Acts 1:20. Then, all other forms of the word "lead" appear 217 times in the NIV (Bible Study Tools, 2024). Also, in comparison, in the English Standard Version (ESV), leadership is only found one time – in Numbers 33:1. Then, all other forms of the word "lead" appear 204 times in the ESV (Bible Study Tools, 2024; ESV, 2001).

On the other hand, the word "follow" and all other forms of this word, such as "follower," can be found 258 times in the KJV (Ritenbaugh, 2024). All forms of "follow" can be found 202 times in the NIV and 273 times in the ESV (Bible Study Tools, 2024; ESV, 2001). "The words 'servant,' 'service,' and 'serve,' in various forms, occur well over 1,100 times in the New International Version. People are servants of other human beings or servants of God" (Elwell, 1997). Then, all forms of the word "serve" and "servant" can be found 1,223 times in the ESV (Bible Study Tools, 2024; ESV, 2001).

When considering how "good" or "great" leadership is defined in Scripture, our understanding must be viewed through a different lens from what is often interpreted to be "good" or "great" throughout human history. Leaders throughout history who had "great" attached to their names were often miserable and flawed, and the validity of their legacy can easily be called into question. Those they ruled were typically unhappy, abused, and mistreated too. Leaders such as Alexander, Catherine, Constantine, Darius, Frederick, Genghis Khan, Peter, Ramses, and others have had the name "great" attributed to them because of their power, influence, expansion of borders, squashing of one's enemies, accomplishments, and more. Much of this approach to how leaders are viewed grew out of the *Great Man Theory* created by Thomas Carlyle in the nineteenth century (Villanova, 2015).

Jesus called out these leaders when speaking to his disciples in Matthew 20:25-26a. He said, "You know that the rulers of the Gentiles *lord it over them*, and their great ones exercise authority over them. *It shall not be this way among you*." [italicized emphasis added] "Too often, our leaders' actions leave us wondering if being a great leader is even possible, or is if the term "great leader" is just another oxymoron? Whether you find yourself confused by the actions of those in charge or coming into a new leadership position yourself, the Bible is full of insight about the kind of leader that God calls us to be and the responsibilities we have even when we're not in charge" (DeWeil, 2024). DeWeil goes on to capture five descriptions of Biblical leadership, all present throughout Scripture from Genesis to Revelation and also evidenced in the life and ministry of Jesus. Each of these descriptions identified by DeWeil is further explored in Chapter 8: The Master Leader's Example:

- A leader honors and submits to God's authority.
- A leader serves.
- A leader knows and cares for their people.
- A leader can be of any age.
- A leader is someone you want to follow.

A LITMUS TEST FROM JAMES

In Scripture, the letter of James discusses the dangers and consequences of a tongue that is out of control and the need to be tamed. Consider the implications of this passage, especially as it relates to leaders. Here are verses 3-10 from this chapter, with emphasis added.

[3] If we put bits into the mouths of horses so that they obey us, we guide their whole bodies as well. [4] Look at the ships also: though they are so large and are driven by strong winds, they are guided by a very small rudder wherever the will of the pilot directs. [5] So also the tongue is a small member, yet it boasts of great things.

How great a forest is set ablaze by such a small fire! [6] And *the tongue is a fire, a world of unrighteousness.* The tongue is set among our members, staining the whole body, setting on fire the entire course of life, and set on fire by hell. [7] For every kind of beast and bird, of reptile and sea creature, can be tamed and has been tamed by mankind, [8] but no human being can tame the tongue. *It is a restless evil, full of deadly poison.* [9] With it we bless our Lord and Father, *and with it we curse people who are made in the likeness of God.* [10] From the same mouth come blessing and cursing. My brothers, these things ought not to be so.

One of the most ridiculous statements from my childhood was that "sticks and stones will break my bones, but words will never hurt me." What a bold-faced, absurd lie! So much hurt can come from what is said to us, especially from those in leadership positions. The tongue is a fire, a world of unrighteousness, a restless evil, and a deadly poison. It is used to curse people who are made in the likeness of God. These are sobering statements from James for those in leadership and authority. We have the ability and opportunity to bless and build up or to curse and destroy, whether these choices are made subtly or not, and whether it is one instance in time or done consistently.

Scripture has much to say about the dangers of gossip

and slander and the intent and tone beyond the words used. While it is tempting to insert some personal stories here of how leaders in the past have cut me down, I have to remind myself, as I am sure you do, too, of the forgiveness, healing, and promises from Scripture. Who Christ says I am speaks louder than the insults hurled at you and me. Also, as leaders, let us be careful about the actions we take toward others with no words or explanation given. These situations can have a significant negative impact and hurt, too.

Then, notice that this same chapter in James ends with a description of wisdom and its connection to our walk with God and our relationships with others, which can surely relate to leadership. James writes in 3:17-18:

> [17] But the wisdom from above is first pure, then peaceable, gentle, open to reason, full of mercy and good fruits, impartial and sincere. [18] And a harvest of righteousness is sown in peace by those who make peace.

Read those two verses and look at the description again. Wisdom from above is pure, peaceable, open to reason, full of mercy and good fruits, impartial and sincere. A great, self-evaluatory litmus test is found in this passage, and as a result, some great questions can be asked to assess your leadership:

1. Are you pure in your intentions, requests, and expectations?
2. Are you peaceable, and do you provide an environment that promotes peace?
3. Are you gentle at all times with how you speak to people, respond to people, etc.?

4. Are you merciful, gracious, and willing to work with others through their hardships, struggles, and learning curves?
5. Are you impartial, and do you treat others without favoritism?
6. Are you sincere?

REFLECT HERE...

Now, did you notice some verses were skipped in James's letter? Go back to the preceding verses in James 3. A stark contrast of description is provided when wisdom is absent in how we live, relate to others, and lead. See verses 14-16 below:

> [14] But if you have bitter jealousy and selfish ambition in your hearts, do not boast and be false to the truth. [15] This is not the wisdom that comes down from above but is earthly, unspiritual, demonic. [16] For where jealousy and selfish ambition exist, there will be disorder and every vile practice.

Bitterness, jealousy, selfish ambition, boasting and pride, dishonest, unspiritual, demonic, disorder, vile practice. Again, though in contrast to James 3:17-18 as previously considered, these preceding verses provide an excellent, self-evaluatory litmus test too, and some great questions can be asked to assess your leadership of others:

1. Are you bitter about someone or something?
2. Are you pursuing things with the wrong ambition and motives?
3. Are you prideful and boastful?
4. Are you honest in your words and actions?
5. Are you experiencing a lack of order and unpleasant situations due to your choices?

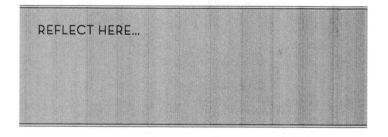

REFLECT HERE...

As author, speaker, and pastor Tony Evans once said, "If you want a better world composed of better countries inhabited by better states that are composed of better counties, made up of better cities that are composed of better neighborhoods, that are illuminated by better churches because they are made up of better families, you see it starts with a better man. It all starts with you and me. It starts with you." The same is true with leadership. Better leadership starts with a better you and me.

Though this chapter has been more reflective, being a good, effective leader starts by exhibiting the characteristics in our lives and how we treat others in James 3:17-18 versus the contrasting characteristics described in James 3:14-16. Often, we have limited control over who is placed in leadership and authority positions and structures above us. Nevertheless, as we lead, we can live the way God calls us to and treat others as we wish.

SPECIFIC PASSAGES AND REFLECTION

Paul wrote to Timothy in the letter of 2 Timothy that Scripture is inspired and is profitable or beneficial for the following: teaching, reproof, correction, and training in righteousness. The New Living Translation says this in 2 Timothy 3:16: "All Scripture is inspired by God and is useful to teach us what is true and to make us realize what is wrong in our lives. It corrects us when we are wrong and teaches us to do what is right." Remember the context of this letter. Paul mentored and reminded Timothy of how to lead others in ministry effectively.

I would be remiss in a chapter on Biblical principles if I failed to provide critical passages from Scripture related to leadership, leading, following, and serving. Allow these passages to do the work of teaching, reproof, correction, and training in righteousness. I encourage you to work through the verses below, and before doing so, pray and ask the Spirit to lead you to the principles that stick out to you. May your reading, reflection, and meditation on God's word not return empty or void, and may it accomplish the purpose for which it was written and sent (Isaiah 55:11).

From Early in the Old Testament

- Exodus 18:21 – Moreover, look for able men from all the people, men who fear God, who are trustworthy and hate a bribe, and place such men over the people as chiefs of thousands, of hundreds, of fifties, and of tens.
- Deuteronomy 1:13 – Choose for your tribes wise, understanding, and experienced men, and I will appoint them as your heads.

- 1 Samuel 16:7 – But the Lord said to Samuel, "Do not look on his appearance or on the height of his stature, because I have rejected him. For the Lord sees not as man sees: man looks on the outward appearance, but the Lord looks on the heart."

From the Proverbs in the Old Testament

- Proverbs 3:5-6 – Trust in the Lord with all your heart, and do not lean on your own understanding. In all your ways acknowledge him, and he will make straight your paths.
- Proverbs 11:14 – Where there is no guidance, a people falls, but in an abundance of counselors there is safety.
- Proverbs 15:22 – Without counsel plans fail, but with many advisers, they succeed.
- Proverbs 16:1-5 – The plans of the heart belong to man, but the answer of the tongue is from the Lord. All the ways of a man are pure in his own eyes, but the Lord weighs the spirit. Commit your work to the Lord, and your plans will be established. The Lord has made everything for its purpose, even the wicked for the day of trouble. Everyone who is arrogant in heart is an abomination to the Lord; be assured, he will not go unpunished.
- Proverbs 16:12-13 – It is an abomination to kings to do evil, for the throne is established by righteousness. Righteous lips are the delight of a king, and he loves him who speaks what is right.
- Proverbs 27:23-24 – Know well the condition of your flocks, and give attention to your herds, for riches

do not last forever; and does a crown endure to all generations?

- Proverbs 29:2 – When the righteous increase, the people rejoice, but when the wicked rule, the people groan.
- Proverbs 29:14 – If a king faithfully judges the poor, his throne will be established forever.

From Later in the Old Testament

- Isaiah 32:1 – Behold, a king will reign in righteousness, and princes will rule in justice. Each will be like a hiding place from the wind, a shelter from the storm, like streams of water in a dry place, like the shade of a great rock in a weary land.
- Micah 6:8 – He has told you, O man, what is good; and what does the Lord require of you but to do justice, and to love kindness, and to walk humbly with your God?

From the Gospels and Acts in the New Testament

- Matthew 20:25-28 – But Jesus called them to him and said, "You know that the rulers of the Gentiles lord it over them, and their great ones exercise authority over them. It shall not be so among you. But whoever would be great among you must be your servant, and whoever would be first among you must be your slave, even as the Son of Man came not to be served but to serve, and to give his life as a ransom for many."

- Matthew 23:11-12 – The greatest among you shall be your servant. Whoever exalts himself will be humbled, and whoever humbles himself will be exalted.
- Matthew 23:1-7 – Then Jesus said to the crowds and to his disciples, "The scribes and the Pharisees sit on Moses' seat, so do and observe whatever they tell you, but not the works they do. For they preach but do not practice. They tie up heavy burdens, hard to bear, and lay them on people's shoulders, but they themselves are not willing to move them with their finger. They do all their deeds to be seen by others. For they make their phylacteries broad and their fringes long, and they love the place of honor at feasts and the best seats in the synagogues and greetings in the marketplaces and being called rabbi by others.
- Luke 6:31 – And as you wish that others would do to you, do so to them.
- Luke 22:26-27 – But not so with you. Rather, let the greatest among you become as the youngest, and the leader as one who serves. For who is the greater, one who reclines at the table or one who serves? Is it not the one who reclines at the table? But I am among you as the one who serves.
- Acts 6:3 – Therefore, brothers, pick out from among you seven men of good repute, full of the Spirit and of wisdom, whom we will appoint to this duty.
- Acts 20:28 – Pay careful attention to yourselves and to all the flock, in which the Holy Spirit has made you overseers, to care for the church of God, which he obtained with his own blood.

From Paul's Letters to Churches
in the New Testament

- Romans 12:3-6a – For by the grace given to me I say to everyone among you not to think of himself more highly than he ought to think, but to think with sober judgment, each according to the measure of faith that God has assigned. For as in one body we have many members, and the members do not all have the same function, so we, though many, are one body in Christ, and individually members one of another. Having gifts that differ according to the grace given to us, let us use them:

- Romans 13:1 – Let every person be subject to the governing authorities. For there is no authority except from God, and those that exist have been instituted by God.

- Ephesians 4:11-13 – And he gave the apostles, the prophets, the evangelists, the shepherds and teachers, to equip the saints for the work of ministry, for building up the body of Christ, until we all attain to the unity of the faith and of the knowledge of the Son of God, to mature manhood, to the measure of the stature of the fullness of Christ,

- Philippians 2:3-4 – Do nothing from selfish ambition or conceit, but in humility count others more significant than yourselves. Let each of you look not only to his own interests, but also to the interests of others.

- Colossians 3:12-13 – Put on then, as God's chosen ones, holy and beloved, compassionate hearts, kindness, humility, meekness, and patience, bearing with one another and, if one has a complaint against another, forgiving each other; as the Lord has forgiven you, so you also must forgive.

- Colossians 3:22-24 – Bondservants, obey in everything those who are your earthly masters, not by way of eye-service, as people-pleasers, but with sincerity of heart, fearing the Lord. Whatever you do, work heartily, as for the Lord and not for men, knowing that from the Lord you will receive the inheritance as your reward. You are serving the Lord Christ.

- 1 Timothy 3:1-4a – The saying is trustworthy: If anyone aspires to the office of overseer, he desires a noble task. Therefore, an overseer must be above reproach, the husband of one wife, sober-minded, self-controlled, respectable, hospitable, able to teach, not a drunkard, not violent but gentle, not quarrelsome, not a lover of money. He must manage his own household well,

- 1 Timothy 4:12 – Let no one despise you for your youth, but set the believers an example in speech, in conduct, in love, in faith, in purity.

- 2 Timothy 2:15 – Do your best to present yourself to God as one approved, a worker who has no need to be ashamed, rightly handling the word of truth.

- 2 Timothy 2:24-25a – And the Lord's servant must not be quarrelsome but kind to everyone, able to teach, patiently enduring evil, correcting his opponents with gentleness.

- Titus 2:7-8 – Show yourself in all respects to be a model of good works, and in your teaching show integrity, dignity, and sound speech that cannot be condemned, so that an opponent may be put to shame, having nothing evil to say about us.

From Other Letters in the New Testament

- Hebrews 13:7 – Remember your leaders, those who spoke to you the word of God. Consider the outcome of their way of life and imitate their faith.
- Hebrews 13:17 – Obey your leaders and submit to them, for they are keeping watch over your souls, as those who will have to give an account. Let them do this with joy and not with groaning, for that would be of no advantage to you.
- James 4:10-11a – Humble yourselves before the Lord, and he will exalt you. Do not speak evil against one another, brothers.
- 1 Peter 5:2-4 – Shepherd the flock of God that is among you, exercising oversight, not under compulsion, but willingly, as God would have you; not for shameful gain, but eagerly; not domineering over those in your charge, but being examples to the flock. And when the chief Shepherd appears, you will receive the unfading crown of glory.

Just from these selected passages above, and there are many more from the pages of Scripture when I spent a lengthy amount of time reading and meditating on them, seven principles of leadership are evident:

1. Great leaders choose to be servants first and care about their "flock."
2. A leader's credibility is tied to how they uphold truth, fairness, and impartiality.
3. Leaders choose to see the best in those who work for them, and they empower them to be better.

4. Leaders are listeners, willing to take advice and criticism to grow and develop.
5. Leaders are humble and willing to put the needs of others before their own.
6. Leaders have exceptional qualities that others recognize and imitate.
7. Leaders act with integrity and set high standards for themselves and others.

What observations do you have from the Scriptures listed in this chapter?

REFLECT HERE...

FINAL THOUGHTS FOR THIS CHAPTER

Scripture provides a beautiful glimpse of what good, positive, spirit-filled, godly leadership should look like. However, as we explored in Chapter 1, not all leaders act and treat their people this way. Some leaders do not have the mind of Christ, as they have not yet chosen to commit their life to Jesus, and as a result, seek to follow and honor Him with their lives, which affects not only who they are as individuals but also how they lead. Also, some leaders claim to know Christ but are either Christians in name only or are not walking in a manner worthy of the gospel (Ephesians 4:1).

Again, as mentioned in Chapter 1, the beauty of the gospel and this book is that it is the heart of God for all to know Him and to live for Him, and we as leaders, though imperfect, choose to either have a positive effect on the lives of others we lead, or a destructive effect. In the next chapter, we work through the five bad leadership characters.

REFLECT HERE ON CHAPTER THOUGHTS, REACTIONS, RESPONSES, ACTION ITEMS...

CHAPTER FIVE

UNPACKING THE FIVE BAD LEADERSHIP CHARACTERS

In Chapter One, an introduction to the five bad leadership characters was briefly described and generally defined. Bad, ineffective leaders are all around us. Some leaders seem to embody pure evil, while some may have good intentions, but the characteristics they exhibit in their leadership are bad and ineffective. As aforementioned, all humanity is fallen and flawed, but there can be hope and redemption amidst this reality. From a Biblical perspective, we have foundational truths that describe good, effective leadership. There are plenty of bad, ineffective examples in Scripture, too. Chapter Seven will further explore these good and bad examples from Scripture.

While bad, ineffective leaders could be categorized in a variety of ways, the Five Bad Leadership Characters described in this book have been formed as a result of extensive interviews, countless conversations and discussions, and reading of stories from history and Scripture (captured in Chapter Seven), as well as from milling through contemporary submissions of stories, some of which form the basis of Chapter Eight. As shared in Chapter One, you have likely worked for one or more of the following characters throughout your life. Additionally, it is worth noting that some bad, ineffective leaders likely share characteristics of more than one of the five characters explained below. The general description of each character is provided again and then unpacked with more real-life examples and stories of what each character might look like and do in their attempts at leadership.

The most challenging part of putting this book together was reading the stories submitted and the devastating effects that bad, ineffective leaders had on contributors' lives. Amidst these probably upsetting stories, sadly, it did allow these Five Bad Leadership Characters to take shape. Additionally, while developing and writing this chapter, two songs came to mind: *Push* by Matchbox Twenty and *Numb* by Linkin Park. So many of the lyrics of these songs describe the adverse actions taken by others against us and the feelings that can come over us due to the adverse treatment. I would encourage you to look up the full lyrics online of these two songs, and portions of each song are provided below. Poor, ineffective leaders have likely led you to feel the emotions of this song, including but not limited to never feeling like you are good enough, feeling like your head will cave in from the stress and toxicity, feeling pushed around, abused, and betrayed, and feeling taken for granted.

Push – Matchbox Twenty

> She said "I don't know if I've ever been good enough...
> I wanna push you around...
> I wanna push you down...
> I wanna take you for granted...
> 'Cause I've been cheated, I've been wronged.
> And you, you don't know me...
> Oh, but don't bowl me over.
> Just wait a minute, well I kinda fell apart...

Numb – Linkin Park

> I'm tired of being what you want me to be
> Feeling so faithless, lost under the surface
> Don't know what you're expecting of me...
> Every step that I take is another mistake to you...
> Can't you see that you're smothering me
> Holding too tightly, afraid to lose control?
> 'Cause everything that you thought I would be
> Has fallen apart right in front of you

Pause for a moment and reflect on the lyrics of these two songs. What stood out and resonated with you? What points do you agree with? What points do you disagree with? What statements could use further investigation for your leadership development?

REFLECT HERE...

THE VILE WITCH DEFINED

These leaders are typically more toward the top of the leadership hierarchy but can also be found in middle-level management. They seem to do everything possible to "I'll get you my pretty," like Elphaba, one of the wicked witches from the book *Wicked: The Life and Times of the Wicked Witch of the West (Wicked Years, 1)*, or the film, *The Wonderful Wizard of Oz* (MacGuire, 2000). They could care less about anyone's needs under them. They do not listen, model next to nothing positive, feel threatened by anyone who asks questions, throw their weight around like a Machiavellian bull in a china shop, harass employees through intimidation, yells to be heard and get their way, stand over others with a wagging finger, and are paranoid that someone might expose their lack of character, skills, and ethics.

The Vile Witch in Action

Here are some quotes and statements from those who contributed to this book that illustrate the nature of The Vile Witch.

- At a recent end-of-the-year ceremony to recognize employees' achievements in my department, my boss recognized everyone except me, including employees who failed in their job responsibilities and resigned before finishing their contract. For some of my colleagues I talked to later, it felt like I was invisible regardless of my fantastic job performance and consistently volunteering to help others and our customers.

- I developed a piece to publish, which is required for my performance evaluation. Because of my heavy workload, I could not move forward quickly with publication, and my boss stole my idea and is now using it as their own to get it published.

- My boss has sought to eradicate all good done by their predecessor. Our department was doing so well until they came in. Now I wonder if my boss is intentionally trying to run off everyone, including our customers, who heavily depend on our department.

- My boss forced out all the top employees in my department and replaced them with subpar employees. As if this was not bad enough, all new employees were directly hired by my boss or promoted from within, and they do not have the qualifications and experience of those who were let go.

- My boss made false allegations about me to get my colleagues to turn against me. They even shared these lies with our customers, ruining my credibility and standing with them.

- My boss changed the duties found in my job description without any conversations, notifications, or warnings. I came in one day, and my job had changed, which was illegal per our organization's policy manual, but I was too exhausted to take on the challenge.

- Though I met all required areas for my performance evaluation standards, my boss demoted me on a made-up technicality.

- My boss has claimed to be an expert in specific topics, but whenever they have been asked about these areas, they suddenly cannot remember, get defensive, and later send terse emails.
- My boss came into their first meeting yelling out commands and expectations without any introductions or knowing who they were meeting with.
- My boss shut down a department in my company without warning, leaving me without a job and our customers stranded with no other service options.
- My boss was so threatened by someone who worked for her that she did everything possible to make this colleague's life miserable by scheduling her outside her regular work shift on weekdays and even required her to come in on weekends when no one else was needed to work.
- My boss was jealous of one of my colleagues who was younger, prettier, and honestly had better people skills. Fearing that my colleague would be liked less, my boss went to the extreme of buying new clothing and jewelry to impress others.

Essential Questions Check-In

For The Vile Witch character, reflect on your experience(s). Have you encountered this bad leadership character, and if so, what was it like? What did you learn, or what can you learn from being under their leadership?

In Chapter 1, you were introduced to the Essential Questions to Ask, so now pause and review the statements about The Vile Witch character. Choose one or two of the bulleted scenarios, personally place yourself in the scenarios, and ask the following:

1. How would you have handled the situation?
2. How could the situation have been handled differently?
3. And most importantly, what can be learned from the situation?

REFLECT HERE...

THE SUCK UP LAPDOG DEFINED

These leaders are typically in middle-level management, and to stay in their position, they usually surrender their soul and well-being to a Vile Witch, Shady Sleaze, or Pontius Pilate Sideliner-type leader above them. Rather than providing care and support for those under them, they only care about pleasing and doing their boss's wishes. Their soul is sold to evil, and they have little to no established trust with others working for/with them because their only concern is to keep the boss happy. This leader may be clueless about their job responsibilities, but because of the constant suck-up to their boss, job security never seems to be a concern.

The Suck Up Lapdog in Action

Here are some quotes and statements from those who contributed to this book that illustrate the nature of The Suck Up Lapdog.

- Somehow, my immediate supervisor failed at doing three separate roles in multiple departments, but because he/she sucked up to leadership, he/she is still at the company.
- My boss abandoned all developed rapport previously held with colleagues and customers to give blind allegiance to their boss. This person who once had our backs suddenly ignored us and sided with their boss instead, even amidst mistreatments.
- My boss no longer spends time with my colleagues and customers; they have lost touch with our personal and professional needs.
- Someone in the organization asked my boss to let me go, but it was clear he was not supportive of the decision. Sadly, rather than advocate and support me, he chose to follow the directives he was given.
- As a part of our company's evaluation and continuous improvement cycle, my boss shut down the opportunity to collect feedback and conduct strategic planning for fear that it might make him/her and their immediate supervisor look bad.
- I was replaced by my boss and replaced with a much less prepared and experienced colleague who was only placed in my previous position because of their relationship with my boss and their family.

- Some of my colleagues, who are poor at their responsibilities, only choose to do a better job when nearing their formal evaluation.

Essential Questions Check-In

For The Suck Up Lapdog character, reflect on your own experience(s). Have you encountered this bad leadership character, and if so, what was it like? What did you learn, or what can you learn from being under their leadership?

Next, do the same for this character with the essential questions. Choose one or two of the bulleted scenarios, personally place yourself in the scenarios, and ask the following:

1. How would you have handled the situation?
2. How could the situation have been handled differently?
3. And most importantly, what can be learned from the situation?

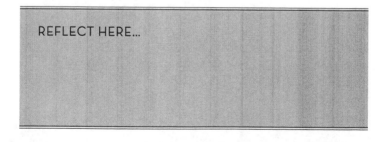

REFLECT HERE...

THE "OH NO!" I AM IN OVER MY HEAD, DEFINED

These leaders typically have no idea how to lead or think they know what they are doing when they do not. They can be found at all levels of management. They possess little to no evidence, skill, or experience of knowing how to lead, build a team or community, or buy in, and it is evident to everyone except them that they are clearly in over their head for the job. They somehow have created an aura  around them that they believe they know what they are doing when, in fact, they have no clue. They are often poor communicators, get upset when questions come, and try to hide from others, especially those working under them, so their ineffectiveness cannot be discovered.

The "Oh No!" I Am in Over My Head in Action

Here are some quotes and statements from those who contributed to this book that illustrate the nature of The "Oh No!" I Am in Over My Head.

- My boss consistently overly depends on others to help do their job well because they are inept, and both know how to do their job and are out of touch with our job duties and responsibilities.

- My boss is never around and visible to employees and customers, leading many to believe they are too scared to be approached.
- After working in my company for a few years, a colleague asked who our boss was because she was absent and out of touch with our department.
- My boss had such an overbearing direct supervisor that he/she was only a mouthpiece versus someone with their leadership, thoughts, and opinions.
- My boss received word that there were some concerns within my department, and rather than working collectively toward a resolution, they killed my department, resulting in some employees losing their jobs or being reassigned elsewhere within the company.
- My boss rearranged her schedule to only come to the office three days a week instead of the required five, leaving my colleagues and me to wonder if they do not know what they are doing and are over their heads.

Essential Questions Check-In

For The "Oh No" I Am in Over My Head character, reflect on your experience(s). Have you encountered this bad leadership character, and if so, what was it like? What did you learn, or what can you learn from being under their leadership?

Next, do the same for this character with the essential questions. Choose one or two of the bulleted scenarios, personally place yourself in the scenarios, and ask the following:

1. How would you have handled the situation?
2. How could the situation have been handled differently?
3. And most importantly, what can be learned from the situation?

REFLECT HERE...

THE SHADY SLEAZE DEFINED

These leaders creep out everyone except those lucky or disillusioned enough to be in their inner circle. They, too, can be found at all levels of management. Somehow, they feel they are above the law, the rules and institutional policies do not apply to them, and they can do whatever they wish. They blur the lines of morals, ethics, and the rule of law. They only care about creepily creating an inner circle of loyalty through whatever means, ethically or not, and intentionally create an "us versus them" mentality in an organization. They hide behind mistruths and pretend to be genuine when, in fact, they are one step away from corruption, scandal, or indictment (or possibly are already in these devastating ends and have not yet been unmasked).

The Shady Sleaze in Action

Here are some quotes and statements from those who contributed to this book that illustrate the nature of The Shady Sleaze.

- My boss has consistently brought in unqualified people to serve in roles in my department, which has led to an exodus of good, qualified people and a decline in customer satisfaction and revenue.
- My boss blatantly ignores established policies for promoting employees in our organization.
- My boss demands loyalty from them and threatens others if they question authority.
- My boss once told me their negative feelings about one of my colleagues and what was planned to rid the company of this colleague.
- My boss has prevented the most qualified candidates from being hired in job search processes for fear that these new people will do too good of a job.
- My boss told me I would receive certain job benefits and incentives, only to say they forgot about ever having this conversation.
- My boss has observed programs and departments struggling in my organization and does nothing. Furthermore, this same boss goes the extra mile to help other departments.

- My boss knowingly broke company policy, contracts, and state law by attempting to force me to sign a new contract for a significant salary reduction.
- After telling my colleagues and me there was no money for doing extras to support our customers and letting some employees go, suddenly money was available at twice the amount to be given to the employees they liked.
- My boss, fearing that I was becoming too popular with our customers, made up a new policy to demote me, thus removing me from having direct contact with our customers.
- When things were becoming unbearable in my job, and I wanted to perform my required duties and responsibilities successfully, I made a list of concerns to share with my boss. When I shared my list, my boss verbally attacked me for putting the list together and did nothing to address my concerns.
- My boss always tells us what to do with our schedules, duties, and responsibilities, but they never do what they ask.
- My boss was not appropriately vetted by mid-level management to come into her position. The policy to bring in my boss was ignored, but now we are stuck with them.

Essential Questions Check-In

For The Shady Sleaze character, reflect on your experience(s). Have you encountered this bad leadership character, and if so, what was it like? What did you learn, or what can you learn from being under their leadership?

Next, do the same for this character with the essential questions. Choose one or two of the bulleted scenarios, personally place yourself in the scenarios, and ask the following:

1. How would you have handled the situation?
2. How could the situation have been handled differently?
3. And most importantly, what can be learned from the situation?

REFLECT HERE...

THE PONTIUS PILATE SIDELINER DEFINED

These leaders typically know what is going on in an organization and may even be attuned to the pulse and culture of the concerns and issues within the organization; however, rather than choosing to step in to be a positive solution to provide support and help to employees and customers, these leaders sadly stay on the sideline and do not actively get involved. They are often found toward the top of the leadership hierarchy. As the Roman leader of this name did, when he had the power to release Jesus because he found no fault or wrong in Jesus, these leaders washed their hands of any sticky or difficult situations. They often place too much blind trust in the ineffective leaders working under them, possibly because they do not care or are so nonconfrontational that they are frightened by others or situations that may be threatening or challenging. They knowingly allow those in leadership to do whatever they wish, and they have little to no commitment to accountability and responsibility. At times, these leaders leave an organization, and the wake of destruction is then fully realized after their departure, and the organization is left to clean up the mess.

The Pontius Pilate Sideliner in Action

Here are some quotes and statements from those who contributed to this book that illustrate the nature of The Pontius Pilate Sideliner.

- My boss knowingly allows for a toxic work environment to exist and, after repeated complaints from colleagues and customers, does nothing.
- My boss is disingenuous with employees who come to them with concerns and do nothing.
- My boss has received customer complaints about employees' wrongdoing and does nothing.
- My boss has received complaints from customers about the mistreatment of employees by mid-level management and does nothing.
- My boss has received formal grievances through proper chains of command as outlined in our company's policy manual but does nothing.

- My boss knows that lower levels of leadership are losing good people and doing nothing.
- My boss knows customers are taking their business elsewhere and does nothing.
- My boss knows that lower levels of leadership mistreat employees and customers, and they do nothing.
- I have a coworker who often fails at their job responsibilities. Colleagues and customers are constantly upset at this coworker, but our boss never does anything to address our concerns and fix the problem.
- My boss has chosen to leave my company in disarray to pursue other personal opportunities rather than right the ship and improve the company before leaving.
- My boss knew that my direct supervisor had broken the law by forcing me to sign a new contract, but rather than holding that supervisor responsible, he did nothing.
- My boss knew that my direct supervisor effectively killed my department, losing good employees, many customers, and revenue, and did nothing.
- My boss got upset that I was not doing my job well after placing me in charge of a department without the proper personnel or financial resources to be successful.

Essential Questions Check-In

For The Pontius Pilate character, reflect on your experience(s). Have you encountered this bad leadership character, and if so, what was it like? What did you learn, or what can you learn from being under their leadership?

Next, do the same for this character with the essential questions. Choose one or two of the bulleted scenarios, personally place yourself in the scenarios, and ask the following:

1. How would you have handled the situation?
2. How could the situation have been handled differently?
3. And most importantly, what can be learned from the situation?

REFLECT HERE...

CONCLUDING THINGS TO PONDER

In the past or present, do you feel the emotions exhibited in the songs *Push* by Matchbox Twenty or *Numb* by Lincoln Park? I cannot even imagine the depths of hurt and pain behind the quotes in the Five Bad Leadership Characters. What is even more upsetting is that some of the quotes and stories above were experienced by people at the hands of religious organizations, which likely includes the three categories of leaders described in Chapter 1: Non-Christians, Christians in name only, and Christians.

How devastating it is that with Christian leaders or in

Christian organizations, these types of behaviors and actions are permitted. One anonymous contributor to this book said that they would never work in a Christian organization again because of the mistreatment and toxicity they faced. They said he has been treated better by non-Christian leaders in secular companies.

Dear reader, it should not be this way! But again, remember the goal of this book, as tempting as it may be. It is not to seek revenge but to see what can be learned from the good, the bad, and the ugly of poor, ineffective leadership. Next, we turn our attention to historical examples of bad leadership, including figures from Scripture.

REFLECT HERE ON CHAPTER THOUGHTS, REACTIONS, RESPONSES, ACTION ITEMS...

CHAPTER SIX

EXAMPLES OF BAD LEADERSHIP FROM HISTORY AND SCRIPTURE

The five bad leadership characters from the previous chapter are not only present and future realities. These characters have existed in the past, too. Some of the historical examples in this chapter may cause you to pause and reflect for a moment, too. You might feel an urge to disagree. While many examples are provided in this chapter, greater attention is given to characters from Scripture. However, dear reader, keep in mind the goal of this book. We are all flawed, and even the best historical characters have flaws and weaknesses, too. Many of these leaders are even memorialized amidst their shortcomings. We can indeed learn from their example of bad, ineffective leadership.

BRIEF MENTION OF HISTORICALLY BAD LEADERS

Throughout history, some prominent bad leaders have likely been familiar to you. Conduct an Internet search of the worst leaders in history, and depending on how long the source's list goes (Top 10, 25, 100, etc.), the figures below will likely appear on your list. From the past 100 years or so, bad political leaders could include the likes of the following leaders:

- Adolf Hitler (Germany)
- Osama Bin Laden (al-Qaida)
- Mengistu Haile Mariam (Ethiopia)
- Joseph Stalin (Soviet Union)
- Mao Zedong (China)
- Kim Il-Sung, Kim Jong Il, and Kim Jong Un (North Korea)
- Fidel Castro (Cuba)
- Saddam Hussein (Iraq)
- Ayatollah Khomeini (Iran)
- Muammar Gaddafi (Libya)
- Idi Amin (Uganda)
- Pol Pot (Cambodia)
- Hideki Tojo (Japan)

Pause and reflect for a moment on two things. First, do you know or think you know about the people mentioned above, and second, who in recent history may be missing from this list?

REFLECT HERE...

Then, travel back further in history, and others may stand out, including the likes of the following leaders:

- Attila the Hun (Germanic Kingdoms)
- Genghis Khan (Mongols)
- Vlad the Impaler (Wallachia, which is now Romania)
- Emperors Nero and Caligula (Roman Empire)
- King Leopold II (Congo)
- Ivan the Terrible (Russia)
- Tiglath Pileser III and Ashurbanipal (Assyrians)
- King John (England)
- Maximillian Robespierre (France)
- Andrew Jackson (US President)
- Talaat Pasha (Ottomans)

Again, pause and reflect on the same two questions from above. First, do you know or think you know about the people mentioned above? Second, throughout history before ca. 1900, who else may be missing from this list?

REFLECT HERE...

CHARACTER SKETCHES FROM SCRIPTURE

Remember, we are all flawed, and just like the leaders mentioned in the previous section, even the best of characters from Scripture had their flaws and weaknesses, too. We can and should learn from their example of bad, ineffective leadership and how, amidst their flaws, God still used them for great purposes. Following each person's sketch below, I encourage you to take a moment to ponder what can be learned in your own life, and specifically in the roles and responsibilities of leaders that you carry.

- *Eve* – Her downfall was eating a fruit from the only tree in the Garden of Eden that God instructed her not to eat. With her husband, Adam, by her side, she listened to bad advice from the serpent, allowed herself to be tempted and tricked, and did the wrong thing. She ate the fruit. When God asked her the reason for her choice, her response was to blame the crafty serpent instead of taking responsibility for her choice.
- *Adam* – Again, that one forbidden tree in the Garden. She was with Eve, and rather than walking away from the temptation or taking steps to redirect his beloved wife from eating the fruit, he stood with her and participated in eating the fruit. They did this action together. Then, when asked by God what happened and why, he did not want to take responsibility for his choice. Then, like Eve, he shifted the blame to his wife, who was the problem, instead of him.
- *Cain* – He became so paranoid and jealous of his brother, Abel, and the sacrifice offered to God by Abel that he went to the ultimate extreme and committed murder. Paranoia, jealousy, discontent – these festered and led him to commit an unspeakable crime – premeditated murder.

- *Abraham* – When he found himself in difficult situations, he lied on more than one occasion to seek favor and approval from others rather than be honest and transparent about his standing and situation. In doing so, he also brought potential danger to those around him.

- *Sarah* – When she was presented with a difficult situation, being too old and barren to conceive and have a child, and the promise of a fantastic miracle in her future, she doubted and laughed aloud at what she thought to be downright ridiculous and impossible.

- *Moses* – On multiple occasions, he lost his cool – once killing an Egyptian who was mistreating someone else and later hitting a rock in the wilderness in front of the entire community when given directions to do otherwise to provide for the basic needs of the people he was leading. He also had an "I can't" mindset, made up excuses and gave reasons to defend himself when tasked by God with a significant opportunity to lead the children of Israel from Egypt to the Promised Land.

- *Aaron* – On the journey to the Promised Land, he became impatient at Mount Sinai. As a response, he led the entire nation to create an idol of a golden calf while they waited for their leader, Moses. Also, he and his sister, Miriam, were quite the complainers about the leadership and decisions made by Moses, God's choice of leader over them.

- *Rahab* – She was a prostitute. Enough said. However, amidst her lifestyle choices and being poorly viewed by others, she heeded the opportunity to protect the spies scoping out the Promised Land. When Jericho was destroyed, she and her family were saved, and her name made it into the genealogy of Christ.

- ***The Unnamed Spies*** – These ten men were given an excellent opportunity to scout the Promised Land, but they could not see the possibilities of what could happen in their future because of fear. God had already promised this land to his people; their only job was to scope it out and report their findings. Instead, fear and doubt was their choice.

- ***Gideon*** – He made excuses about the unimpressive pedigree of his family and background to be able to contribute and do big things. When given reassurances, he still was not convinced. He needed multiple fleeces and affirmations to feel the courage to lead others to victory. With God's favor, he only needed 300 men and no weapons to defeat the Midianites.

- ***Samson*** – He used his physical strength to get what he wanted and drive fear into his enemies. When that was not enough, he used riddles and trickery to get his way.

- ***Eli*** – He was a high priest called to represent the people before God. However, he made wrong assumptions about others and judged them before knowing the whole story – remember the assumption that Hannah, Samuel's mom, was drunk in the temple even though she was fervently praying for God's favor to provide her with a son? Also, in his position of high priest, he failed to hold his sons accountable (they were priests too, and therefore had leadership responsibilities to carry) for their actions as the Levitical priests of the day.

- ***Saul*** – He was tall and handsome. He was the first king of Israel. He was prone to rage, and he consistently struggled with being paranoid and jealous, especially of David.

- **David** – He was God's chosen king for Israel. He was a shepherd boy who defeated a giant. He was even called a man after God's own heart. However, to get what he wanted related to his lust and sexual desires – remember he saw that beautiful woman, Bathsheba, bathing, he committed sexual sin. Then, to cover up his mistake, he used trickery to harm others – remember Uriah, Bathsheba's husband. David ordered Uriah to be placed on the front line of battle so that he would die.

- **Absolom** – Rather than being content with the leadership placed over him, David, his father, sought to organize a rebellion to stage a coup to take out his father.

- **Solomon** – Yes, he was wise, rich, well-versed, and liked by others, and he expanded his kingdom's territory during his reign. However, he allowed his heart, passion, and direction as a leader to be led away by 1,000+ distractions in sexual sin.

- **Elijah** – After calling down fire from heaven to show God's power on Mount Carmel, thus defeating the priests of Baal and witnessing firsthand what God can miraculously do, afterward, in fear, he ran from this mountaintop moment. He chose to go and sleep under a broom tree in the wilderness, wishing to be dead, fearing that his remaining enemies would find him as he doubted God's favor and protection.

- **Jezebel** – Being so paranoid about anyone who might have a different idea, belief, or dissent, she and her husband, Ahab, had many of the country's leaders killed. Furthermore, she sends letters in her husband's name against innocent people to have them captured and killed.

- **Nebuchadnezzar** – He was so authoritarian that he created a statue, which everyone in the land was required to bow down and worship. When some men named Shadrach, Meshach, and Abednego resisted the directive, Nebuchadnezzar sought to have them killed in a fiery furnace.

- **Darius** – Though he was a wise king, he listened to some ill-advised suggestions from some advising leaders and ended up nearly having his friend, Daniel, killed by lions in a den.

- **Jonah** – He ran from an opportunity before him. He was told to preach to the people of Nineveh, east of where he lived. Instead, he boarded a ship in Joppa and sailed west. He learned his lesson after being thrown overboard in a storm, being swallowed, spending three days in a big fish, and then vomiting onto the shore. He had a second chance to go to Nineveh and saw incredible results of people turning to God, but after having this mountain top high a moment of seeing God work, he had quite a pity party for himself.

- **Herod** – He was so paranoid of anyone challenging his authority, even a newborn baby. So, to prevent the opportunity of a baby rising against him, he had all boys, ages two and under, slaughtered throughout the land.

- **Martha** – Though one of Jesus' dearest friends, she struggled with her to-do list and busied herself with task completion.

- **Thomas** – Though he was one of the disciples of Jesus and spent three years doing ministry with Jesus, he struggled with doubting his leader, asking for proof of nail-scarred hands and feet that Jesus had done what he said he would do following his death.

- *Peter* – Another disciple of Jesus. He was impulsive with his words and actions – remember the suggestion of creating a tent for his leader, Jesus, Elijah, and Moses, instead of only for Jesus at the Transfiguration. Or remember his lack of loyalty in vehemently denying his leader and friend three times and going as far as impulsively cutting off a soldier's ear in the Garden of Gethsemane.

- *Pilate* – He allowed the Messiah, Jesus, the Savior and Creator of the world, who was innocent of any crime, to be publicly beaten, humiliated, and executed through crucifixion. He washed his hands of the opportunity to stand for what was right. He allowed a convicted criminal, Barabbas, off the hook for his crimes and, in doing so, gave the crowds what they wanted, sending Jesus to death. His lack of leadership was so ineffective that one of the five characters of this book is named after him.

- *Paul* – Pre-name change from Saul to Paul; he hunted down others who dissented the religious norms, seeking to take them out through persecution and even death so that they could no longer be a threat.

Essential Questions Check-In

Before proceeding with this chapter, I encourage you to pause, choose two or three of the Biblical characters, personally place yourself in their situation, and ask the following:

1. How would you have handled the situation?
2. How could the situation have been handled differently?
3. And most importantly, what can be learned from the situation?

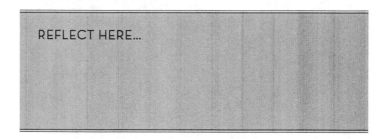

REFLECT HERE...

SOLOMON'S SON, REHOBOAM

While other examples of poor leadership exist throughout Scripture, one stands out. To understand it, we have to go back to the early history of Israel and Judah. Three kings had already ruled the unified country of Israel – Saul, David, and Solomon. However, the nation was in utter disarray and disunity after Solomon's reign. In 1 Kings 11, we read that Solomon's lack of leadership and willfully turning himself and the people led him away from following God; his kingdom was divided in two. Jeroboam would lead the northern tribes of Israel, and Rehoboam, one of Solomon's sons, would rule Judah to the south.

In 1 Kings 12, we read about both men's lousy leadership.

> ¹ Rehoboam went to Shechem, for all Israel had come to Shechem to make him king. ² And as soon as Jeroboam the son of Nebat heard of it (for he was still in Egypt, where he had fled from King Solomon),

then Jeroboam returned from Egypt. ³ And they sent and called him, and Jeroboam and all the assembly of Israel came and said to Rehoboam, ⁴ "Your father made our yoke heavy. Now therefore lighten the hard service of your father and his heavy yoke on us, and we will serve you." ⁵ He said to them, "Go away for three days, then come again to me." So, the people went away.

⁶ Then King Rehoboam took counsel with the old men, who had stood before Solomon his father while he was yet alive, saying, "How do you advise me to answer this people?" ⁷ And they said to him, "If you will be a servant to this people today and serve them and speak good words to them when you answer them, then they will be your servants forever." ⁸ But he abandoned the counsel that the old men gave him and took counsel with the young men who had grown up with him and stood before him. ⁹ And he said to them, "What do you advise that we answer this people who have said to me, 'Lighten the yoke that your father put on us'?" ¹⁰ And the young men who had grown up with him said to him, "Thus shall you speak to this people who said to you, 'Your father made our yoke heavy, but you lighten it for us,' thus shall you say to them, 'My little finger is thicker than my father's thighs. ¹¹ And now, whereas my father laid on you a heavy yoke, I will add to your yoke. My father disciplined you with whips, but I will discipline you with scorpions.'"

¹² So Jeroboam and all the people came to Rehoboam the third day, as the king said, "Come to me again the third day." ¹³ And the king answered the people harshly and forsaking the counsel that the old men had given him, ¹⁴ he spoke to them according

to the counsel of the young men, saying, "My father made your yoke heavy, but I will add to your yoke. My father disciplined you with whips, but I will discipline you with scorpions." [15] So the king did not listen to the people, for it was a turn of affairs brought about by the Lord that he might fulfill his word, which the Lord spoke by Ahijah the Shilonite to Jeroboam the son of Nebat.

Rehoboam, the new leader of Israel, had the opportunity to lead his people well. Amidst his father's poor choices, he had a chance to correct the leadership course and reverse the country's direction. Jeroboam and the people came to Rehoboam with concerns about how they were treated under Solomon's rule. The people felt what was required of them with their work under Solomon was too much to bear. They wanted a lighter load. Rehoboam responded that he would give them a reply in three days. The people surely thought their request would be answered in their favor. Optimistically, they hoped that change would come because they were allowed to share their concerns. Instead, after the promised three days, the exact opposite happened. Rehoboam returned to provide the people with his response after seeking counsel, and here is what he said. "My father made your yoke heavy, but I will add to your yoke. My father disciplined you with whips, but I will discipline you with scorpions."

Rehoboam did not listen to the people. He gave them a sense of false hope that they would be heard. Have you worked for someone who was a demanding boss and taskmaster? Have you received an opportunity to give feedback or ask for a favor, and instead of things becoming more accessible, the boss made things even more complicated?

REFLECT HERE...

To make things worse, Rehoboam's bad leadership was riddled with two other problems, which you may have experienced in working with those in authority. First, he ignored the wise, mature counsel provided to him by those older, who had more context and background to speak to the request and who had the people's best interests in mind. Second, Rehoboam seems to have been on a major ego trip, reminiscent of the qualities and characteristics of one of the five bad leadership characters described in this book, The Vile Witch, who can tend to lead like a bull in a china shop.

Regardless of the possible symbolic meaning in 1 Kings 12:10 and the size of one's "finger," Rehoboam wanted to define and establish who he was and how he would be known and eventually remembered as a leader. He would intentionally be known as ruthless, uncaring, unsympathetic, egotistical, and power-hungry. He would be great, not through God's blessings, humility, and service, but rather as a dictatorial leader who would do everything in his power to be greater than his father and others regardless of the ways and means to get there, and no matter the results of the choices made (N.A., 2018).

FINAL THOUGHTS FOR THIS CHAPTER

Consider how many leaders throughout history, whether in Scripture or not, have become consumed with how great they can be and their legacy being selfish and based on what they acquired through questionable means. You have likely worked for some individuals whose leadership has struggled with this tendency. Being great, one-upping, knocking others off the ladder as we ascend, bootstrap pulling, and getting some airtime and fame time have consumed our culture, and it should not surprise us that some leaders are finished with it as well. Next, we transition to considering contemporary stories of lousy leadership.

REFLECT HERE ON CHAPTER THOUGHTS, REACTIONS, RESPONSES, ACTION ITEMS...

CHAPTER SEVEN

CONTEMPORARY STORIES OF BAD LEADERSHIP

Now that we have considered stories from Scripture and human history, we focus on some contemporary stories of bad, ineffective leadership. Each story in this chapter is a real-life story, graciously submitted by those who contributed to this book. All personal identifiers have been removed for anonymity, and permission has been gathered from each contributor to share their story. Before proceeding with this chapter, I want to thank these special people for the detailed stories submitted for this chapter. You know who you are, and again, thank you.

Following each person's story, opportunities to pause, consider, and respond to the Essential Questions to Ask.

JACK

It was a cold, dreary afternoon in the middle of January. Since Mr. Watson requires all parent meetings to be outside the school day hours, Miss Green (teacher) has rearranged her plans to attend and lead this meeting. Miss Green is not thanked for the personal time she gives up. The meeting takes almost 2 hours. Miss Green does her best to effectively convey the concerns to the parents and work together to produce a plan to help the student, all while Mr. Watson sits behind his computer screen, supposedly taking meeting notes. Miss Green thoroughly goes through the data, breaks down the "teacher terms," and provides specific examples of the student's work, with no input from Mr. Watson.

At the end of the meeting, Mr. Watson decides to provide his input after the parent leaves. With a derogatory tone, Mr. Watson tells Miss Green how there is no way the parents understood anything that Miss Green went over and how the parents are leaving exhausted and confused because Miss Green did not do a good job. Miss Green listens to Mr. Watson respectfully and says ok. Mr. Watson keeps hammering his point home, even though Miss Green does not argue with him. The examples Mr. Watson confuses Miss Green gives, although she does not say anything, because the repercussions of saying something are not worth standing up for herself. Miss Green also wonders why Mr. Watson did not speak up during the meeting if he had these concerns. Mr. Watson says that the parent does not know what "mixed numbers" are and that Miss Green should have explained what those are; Miss Green did explain what those were. Mr. Watson said Miss Green should have shown the parent examples of the student's work; Miss Green brought writing samples that the student had done.

Just relieved to be back in her classroom after getting chewed out from this meeting that had to occur outside of school hours due to Mr. Watson's policy, Miss Green checks her email before leaving for the day. What does she find? The multiple emails Mr. Watson sent out to the staff during the meeting were utterly unrelated to the meeting. It makes sense now that while Mr. Watson's examples confused Miss Green and why Mr. Watson did not speak up during the meeting, Mr. Watson was not just taking meeting notes behind his screen but sending emails and checking off things on his to-do list. This only validated Miss Green's decision not to stand up for herself. Mr. Watson found other things to be more critical than to be invested in that meeting. Oh, and the cherry on top, after receiving the meeting minutes from Mr. Watson, Miss Green had to correct the many spelling and grammar mistakes made by Mr. Watson.

Bad Leadership Character and Essential Questions Check-In

First, ask yourself which of the five bad leadership characters you see present in Jack's story (The Vile Witch, The Suck Up Lapdog, The "Oh No!" I Am in Over My Head, The Shady Sleaze, or The Pontius Pilate Sideliner). Then, personally place yourself in Jack's scenario and ask the following:

1. How would you have handled the situation?
2. How could the situation have been handled differently?
3. And most importantly, what can be learned from the situation?

REFLECT HERE...

KAREN

Over ten years ago, I worked for a mid-sized healthcare organization with leaders I respected and admired when Bob, a new director, was hired to lead a crucial team known for exceeding their objectives. Initially, all seemed well in his first 90 days; then I started noticing red flags; they were small, then they became prominent and treacherous. Bob's sales district went from the top in sales to the middle of the pack. I started noticing that he told lies that were easy to verify, and then he doubled down on them like a popular frat boy bully with the world's most enormous megaphone. He was like George Santos; his lies were blatantly inconsistent, and he retold the same stories with different endings. He liked to drink with senior executives at the bar after meetings. He was always the last one returning to his hotel room. His drinking time with senior executives contributed to their close relationships. They liked him and enjoyed his inappropriate stories about colleagues.

However, this story illustrates Bob's true soul. One day, as I entered the office, I jumped into the elevator as Rob humiliated a colleague due to the size of his lunch box. He asked if he could borrow the lunchbox for his family's picnic. I realized our colleagues in the elevator enjoyed Bob's jokes and fun when they were not his current target. He teased the employee about the entire elevator ride. As we got off the elevator, I said, "Bob, you are a bully," loudly. Then he asked if I wanted the same lunch box. I smiled at the colleague and said YES. Then Bob went in on me.

I smiled and called him an inappropriate anatomical term in front of everyone. He looked like he wanted to punch me. I prayed he would because I was taking kickboxing classes daily, and I wished he would take a swing at me. He did not know I helped boxers practice their defense skills in the ring as they prepared for a match, and they could not punch or kick me. I was unafraid of Bob since I knew I could last three consecutive rounds or nine minutes of punching and kicking before draining half my energy. My frustrations watching Bob terrorize colleagues gave me motivation in the gym. One day after work, during an intense workout, my trainer asked if I wanted revenge because someone stole my lunch money. I smiled and thought about Bob. I realized Bob stole my colleague's self-respect via public humiliation. My office was on the executive row, right down the hall from Bob. Bob's bullying antics entertained senior leaders. However, I viewed him as a micro-aggression and gas lighter. I figured out how to perfect burpees and practiced kicking like Bruce Lee to remove my rage at his disorderly behavior. My daily kickboxing became an outlet for my anger as I worked closely with the vile "mean boy" witch, Bob.

Bob responded to the tragic death of an employee in a very public manner by sharing and resharing her story in work settings while inserting himself a little at a time. Eventually, he began to be the center of her story.

Bob never had a kind word about our boss. He spoke negatively about her and undermined her at every opportunity. I saw what Bob was doing from day one, but it took a while before and our boss saw it. When our boss was diagnosed with stage four breast cancer, he called her three times a week to gain health updates, which he quickly shared with nosey senior leaders internationally. His goal was to gain their acceptance. Bob envied her strategic insight and leadership. He used these frequent wellness checks to ask how she would navigate tricky situations. Bob volunteered to travel globally on behalf of our team; he scheduled dinners with senior executives to share her health progress with this influential audience as he undermined her with the executive leadership team.

Bob inserted himself into her storyline. Her pre-cancer work-related wins became his; the private things she shared about her struggles with cancer were no longer intimate when he shared them with her boss and the executive leadership team. Before her diagnosis, our leader did not trust or like him, yet he became her trusted advisor. He humiliated people in public settings at work and retold the stories like a highly paid comedian. He knew how to work up the crowd. As Bob drank like a frat boy and violated his boss's confidence, he gained the confidence of our senior executive leadership team. My boss could not see how Bob was undermining her. As I warned her, she dismissed my concerns. Eventually, our boss returned to work; unfortunately, she was forced out of the organization in record time. I was promoted to a global role. Bob was promoted to her job and traveled to our headquarters office, where I saw him frequently.

Years later, our boss acknowledged how Bob undermined her. She was angered by how much she trusted him and was abused by Rob. A senior executive told me a story about Bob. He went deer hunting with Bob and left the organization when he could see his true character. He warned me that he had seen pure evil during their hunting weekend, and we quit his job before he had another one. He told me to watch out for Bob because he was vindictive and strongly desired to harm anyone not on his team. He said he never saw pure evil personified in one person until he met Bob. He warned me never to be alone in Bob's presence and always to protect myself.

During international trips, we shared a few one-on-one dinners with Bob while staying at the same company-required hotel during overnight layovers before an early flight home. He always invited me to dinner at the Amsterdam Sheraton Hotel. It offered exceptional meals and service; I used every excuse to avoid his presence. Sometimes, I changed my flights to depart through Germany to avoid being on the same plane and layover schedule since we lived in the same major city. One of Bob's minions still looks at my LinkedIn page weekly. I have blocked him, yet he still accesses my profile to track where I am working. I always felt the negative energy so strong that it kept me on guard. Bob shared Stories where he punished people who were not loyal to him. After these dinners, I called my husband and shared the conversations. My husband feared for my safety during the travel.

God is good. As my career evolved, I led the senior executive assessment centers, and eventually, Bob was assessed by my team of external industrial psychologists. As I shared Bob's assessment results with senior executives, they noticed the unusual patterns and inconsistency with comparative assessments. They expressed concerns about him during our assessment meetings. I carefully chose my words as I shared themes in his evaluation. I shared his lack of alignment with our organizational "people-centered" value and his team's negative engagement results. The senior executives knew something was different about him, but they were under Bob's vile witch spell.

Bob taught me a few lessons:

- Speaking up and talking does not always result in good winning over evil.
- Over time, genuine character flaws are revealed; they may need time and opportunity to become self-evident.
- Trust built on maliciousness and evil contribute to considerable organizational losses. Numerous people are impacted, and the organization's culture is built on the minimum the organization is willing to accept.
- Leaders like Bob are like cancer that spreads quickly and extensively within an organization. Their stories reveal the ineptness and lack of morals in executive leadership.
- Good will always triumph over evil; sometimes, it rules too long, and good people are hurt for revealing the truth.

Bad Leadership Character and Essential Questions Check-In

First, ask yourself which of the five bad leadership characters you see present in Karen's story (The Vile Witch, The Suck Up Lapdog, The "Oh No!" I Am in Over My Head, The Shady Sleaze, or The Pontius Pilate Sideliner). Then, personally place yourself in Karen's scenario and ask the following:

1. How would you have handled the situation?
2. How could the situation have been handled differently?
3. And most importantly, what can be learned from the situation?

REFLECT HERE...

PATTY PAIGE

Over the years, I had quite a few different principals. Each one had her unique style. Some had thought through it quite well; some came to leadership naturally, and some were never a good fit for the position.

My best example of leadership came from one of the last principals I taught under. Mrs. B began as a teacher, moved up to a reading specialist, and then through the ranks of vice principal and principal. She taught me so much about being a quality teacher by her example of excellence as a principal.

She was well aware of what was happening in the classrooms and the atmosphere each teacher cultivated among her children. Bobbye walked the halls of the school each morning and each afternoon. She noticed which classes were quietly working, which were happily engaged in active learning, and which seemed out of control. As she made her rounds, she saw classroom helpers taking a message to the office or bulletin boards that needed to be changed, classroom floors that needed to be picked up, and creative art projects hung for display. Once, when my bulletin board was up just a little too long, she graciously asked if she could help me put up a new one—and she meant it! I changed that bulletin board as soon as possible!

She had four or six lessons about civic responsibility, which she titled "being a good neighbor." Each grading period, she would come into each classroom for a 30-minute interactive lesson about some aspect of getting along well in society. The children were always on their best behavior and seemed happy to see her. From those brief times in the classes, she learned children's names, how they engaged in a lesson, their habits in class, and so on. I learned so much about making a large concept easily accessible to young minds, which was especially helpful since I had moved down from teaching middle school.

As a first-grade teacher, I learned how comprehensive and exhausting teaching that grade could be: it was like having a tub full of water and ping-pong balls and trying to keep all the balls underwater while teaching them something!! Add to that getting all of them through six different levels of books—a recipe for exhaustion. Bobbye understood that and gave us a compassionate ear when needed.

Bobbye was focused, deliberate, and planned. She did not micromanage, from kids' names to teachers' cars, even while noticing details. (She noticed how often I stayed at school quite late to make sure everything was ready for the following day.) She did not expect anything from her teachers that she did not require of herself. She interpreted new state rulings as wisely as possible for different levels. Above all, she was kind, firm, and respectful when needed. She trusted her teachers to do their jobs but was always in charge.

Before she passed away, she had the honor of having an elementary school named after her...an honor well deserved. Great and wise leaders leave an indelible impression on those around them for generations; she was no exception.

Terrible bosses are unpredictable. Often, they wrongly blame employees for the effects of situations they created, e.g., an owner who over-orders stock and then is upset with the employees when they cannot find space to store it all. This is horrible if it happens repeatedly. Bad leadership micromanages, noticing and commenting negatively on all the details. Wise leadership trusts the people they hire and checks up on that respectfully.

Bad leadership exhibits poor character. I had a principal one year who often left early on Friday and came to school inebriated on Monday. Another criticized teachers for being late when he usually arrived right before the bell rang.

Poor leadership: giving an employee a task, then continually interrupting them to do something else.

- Telling a vendor, the store uses how terrible the employees are—in their hearing.
- Issuing checks and telling the employees not to cash them immediately or having the checks bounce. Money management should be the hallmark of good leadership.
- Managing the store or business poorly to the extent that the company is in a precarious position, which all the employees know. That makes them feel insecure and does not inspire respect for the boss.
- Ignoring a whole section of the business, store, etc., and refusing to interact with those employees.
- Refusing to recognize difficulties with the company's functioning and refusing to find ways to rectify them.
- Continually telling employees what to do (or anyone, for that matter!), especially if it is in a quite forceful or demeaning way.
- Being overly critical

Bad Leadership Character and Essential Questions Check-In

First, ask yourself which of the five bad leadership characters you see present in Patty Paige's story (The Vile Witch, The Suck Up Lapdog, The "Oh No!" I Am in Over My Head, The Shady Sleaze, or The Pontius Pilate Sideliner). Then, personally place yourself in Patty Paige's scenario and ask the following:

1. How would you have handled the situation?
2. How could the situation have been handled differently?
3. And most importantly, what can be learned from the situation?

REFLECT HERE...

NOW IT IS YOUR TURN

I know, dear reader, you have a story (or a few or many) to tell. If you were to contribute to the stories such as the ones contained in this book, what would you write? As I shared with you in the opening paragraph of Chapter 1, the inspiration for this book started as a cathartic and therapeutic activity. As I processed my own stories and journey at the hands of bad, ineffective leaders, I quickly realized in conversations with other leaders from a variety of contexts that many in leadership positions (and many not in these positions) have experienced the not-so-good, the bad, and the ugly in the workplace. Again, most of us have been hurt, burned, and mistreated by those in leadership, and sadly, even in religious organizations and businesses. You have likely worked for one or more of the five bad leadership characters: The Vile Witch,

The Suck Up Lapdog, The "Oh No!" I Am in Over My Head, The Shady Sleaze, or The Pontius Pilate Sideliner. Maybe you have worked simultaneously for more than one of these bad leadership characters.

So, before you transition to the closing chapter of this book, it may be a beneficial exercise for you to do some reflection and writing. Even if you do not write anything, talking through and verbally processing your journey as a developing leader and a follower may be highly valuable.

REFLECT HERE...

FINAL THOUGHTS

Experience is a good teacher, and reflecting on even the bad experiences you have likely faced at the hands and influence of a poor, ineffective leader can benefit your soul, mainly if you have never intentionally worked through these negative experiences. There is relief, freedom, and healing possible through casting our cares on Him (God) as he genuinely cares for you. Release the cares, worries, and anxiety of those who have wronged you in leadership and move forward without the burden. Before moving to the next chapter, which focuses on the master leader's example, I close out this chapter by reminding you of the encouragement and promise of 1 Peter 5:7. Take a look at how different versions and translations capture this fantastic verse:

- Cast all your anxiety on Him because he cares for you. (NIV)
- Give all your worries and cares to God, who cares about you. (NLT)
- Casting all your anxieties on Him because he cares for you. (ESV)
- Having cast all your anxiety on Him because He cares about you. (NASB)
- God cares for you, so turn all your worries to Him. (CEV)
- Casting all your cares [all your anxieties, worries, and concerns, once and for all] on Him, for He cares about you [with deepest affection, and watches over you very carefully]. (Amplified)

REFLECT HERE ON CHAPTER THOUGHTS, REACTIONS, RESPONSES, ACTION ITEMS...

CHAPTER EIGHT

THE MASTER LEADER'S EXAMPLE

Building on the cursory look of servant leadership in Chapter 2, the epitome, perfect model of this type of leadership was Jesus. Apologies due to Robert Greenleaf, as it was not your 1973 essay, *The Servant as Leader*. Everything Jesus did was to bring glory to his Father. He did nothing for Himself. Instead, all his teaching, ministry, and relationships built were for others, not Himself. The penultimate example of a servant is described in John 13 when Jesus washes his disciples' feet. Michael (2024a) wrote, "In the Jewish culture of Jesus' time, washing the feet of another man is known to be even humiliating that only the lowliest of enslaved people would perform. Yet Jesus chose to go down on his knees to wash the disciples' feet as a symbol of Him serving them. Ultimately, he sacrificed Himself for the salvation of the world — the ultimate in servitude."

DIRTY FEET, BECOMING A SERVANT, AND SACRIFICE

Before moving forward in this chapter, I want to draw your attention to Michael's (2024a) quote in the previous paragraph. Jesus, the Creator and Savior of the world, came to earth to rescue humanity from their sin and to provide a way for us to get back to God. This Jesus washed his disciples' feet. These were not feet that had just been washed. It was dinner time, so these feet had been walking for many hours up to this point. Jesus took the role of the lowest of servants and did the unthinkable. Possibly for you, even clean feet gross you out. Consider the stink, the layers of dirt, the sweat. Yuck. The Master Leader gets down on his knees to wash not only one disciple's two feet but also He washes all twelve of them, or twenty-four feet in total. Look at the description of this story in John 13:1-17.

> [1] Now before the Feast of the Passover, when Jesus knew that his hour had come to depart out of this world to the Father, having loved his own who were in the world, he loved them to the end. [2] During supper, when the devil had already put it into the heart of Judas Iscariot, Simon's son, to betray him, [3] Jesus, knowing that the Father had given all things into his hands, and that he had come from God and was going back to God, [4] rose from supper. He laid aside his outer garments, and taking a towel, tied it around his waist.
> [5] Then he poured water into a basin and began to wash the disciples' feet and to wipe them with the towel that was wrapped around him. [6] He came to Simon Peter, who said to him, "Lord, do you wash my feet?" [7] Jesus answered him, "What I am doing

you do not understand now, but afterward you will understand." [8] Peter said to him, "You shall never wash my feet." Jesus answered him, "If I do not wash you, you have no share with me."

[9] Simon Peter said to him, "Lord, not my feet only but also my hands and my head!"

[10] Jesus said to him, "The one who has bathed does not need to wash, except for his feet, but is completely clean. And you[b] are clean, but not every one of you." [11] For he knew who was to betray him; that was why he said, "Not all of you are clean."

[12] When he had washed their feet and put on his outer garments and resumed his place, he said to them, "Do you understand what I have done to you? [13] You call me Teacher and Lord, and you are right, for so I am. [14] If I then, your Lord and Teacher, have washed your feet, you also ought to wash one another's feet. [15] For I have given you an example, that you also should do just as I have done to you. [16] Truly, truly, I say to you, a servant is not greater than his master, nor is a messenger greater than the one who sent him. [17] If you know these things, blessed are you if you do them.

Jesus is THE example laid out before us. Paul explained Jesus and his leadership ministry from a dark, lonely prison cell when he wrote his letter to the church at Phillipi. While empathy for a servant leader is simply being able to visualize yourself in someone else's position and understand what someone is feeling, Jesus went even further. Paul wrote the following in Philippians 2:3-8:

[3] Do nothing from selfish ambition or conceit, but in humility count others more significant than

yourselves. [4] Let each of you look not only to his own interests but also to the interests of others. [5] Have this mind among yourselves, which is yours in Christ Jesus [6] who, though he was in the form of God, did not count equality with God a thing to be grasped, [7] but emptied himself, by taking the form of a servant, being born in the likeness of men. [8] And being found in human form, he humbled himself by becoming obedient to the point of death, even death on a cross.

There are some incredible leadership principles contained in these verses. Go back and reread the passage. Here are some takeaways for leaders:

The Good, Effective Leader...

- Is humble
- Sees others as more important than themselves
- Cares more about the interests of others,
- Has the mind of Christ
- Is content being in the place they find themselves
- Is obedient
- Is sacrificial and a servant
- Allows others to get the credit

The Bad, Ineffective Leader comparable to the Five Leadership Characters Identified in This Book...

- Selfish
- Conceited
- Lacks humility
- Is more concerned with themselves versus others

- Only care about their interests
- Does not have the mind of Christ
- Seeks to elevate themselves to a position without merit
- Exalts themselves
- Fills themselves with anything and everything that they need versus what others need

THE FLIPPED SCRIPT

While there are many books on leadership, most do not recognize that Jesus flipped the narrative script on leadership. It is clear from the Gospels that Jesus dealt with the bad leadership characters from Chapter 5 (The Vile Witch, The Suck Up Lapdog, The "Oh No!" I Am in Over My Head, The Shady Sleaze, or The Pontius Pilate Sideliner). During his day, the Pharisees, Sadducees, religious leaders, scribes, Jewish political leaders, and Roman political leaders presented him with challenges, struggles, and difficulties. Leadership throughout human history, from when Jesus was physically on earth to the present, has often been consumed with power, might, and greatness, attracting as many followers as possible and making a name for oneself (Stasek, 2022). However, let us consider what Jesus said about leadership in Matthew 20:25-28. One day, the mother of the sons of Zebedee, James, and John asked Jesus about special privileges for her sons in Jesus' kingdom, and here was his reply:

> [25] But Jesus called them to him and said, "You know that *the rulers of the Gentiles lord it over them*, and their great ones exercise authority over them. [26] It

shall not be so among you. But *whoever would be great among you must be your servant,* [27] and whoever would be first among you must be your slave, [28] even as *the Son of Man came not to be served but to serve, and to give his life* as a ransom for many." [emphasis added]

"Leadership isn't about making our names known. It's about making God's name known and having the ability to love and respect the people in our care, using the authority we've been given with grace" (Stasek, 2022, p. 1). In reflecting on who Jesus is through opportunities and positions of leader, a person should exhibit six characteristics, according to Stasek:

1. Integrity
2. Humility
3. Flexibility
4. Resilience
5. Stewardship
6. Empathy

The Master Leader demonstrated servant leadership throughout his entire time on earth, and with his followers stated, "If anyone wants to be first, he shall be last of all, and servant of all" (Mark 9:35). In doing so, yes, he served. Still, in his serving, he demonstrated much more. He showed true strength, humility, care, value, love for others, and even sacrifice. In his own words, Jesus talked about the ultimate way to serve, which involves sacrificing one's life. After reminding his disciples of the greatest commandment, which he previously told them during his ministry (see Matthew 22:36-40), in John 15:12-13, he said: "This is my commandment, that you love one another as I have loved you. Greater love has no one than this, that someone lay down his life for his friends."

In Chapter 5, the following descriptions of Biblical leadership were captured by DeWeil (2024). All of these are not only present throughout Scripture from Genesis to Revelation but also evidenced in the Master Leader's life and ministry:

- A leader honors and submits to God's authority.
- A leader serves.
- A leader knows and cares for their people.
- A leader can be of any age.
- A leader is someone you want to follow.

While Jesus, The Master Leader, had a mass following during his earthly ministry, two realities were evident:

1. He was dedicated to pouring his life, wisdom, and guidance into a small group of twelve individuals, his disciples.
2. He had enemies, and not everyone agreed with his purpose, message, and mission.

In looking back at the passage from Paul to the Philippians at the beginning of this chapter, one description of The Master Leader is clear. He humbled Himself. Scripture teaches that Jesus was without sin, so the humility described in this letter to the Philippians was not one of needing to humble Himself because of sin. Instead, he chose to take a lower position to serve, and in his service, he decided to make the ultimate sacrifice, to give his life.

SELF-CHECK TIME

Take a moment to do a self-check. In your leadership positions at home, work, church, community, etc., are you serving those with whom you work? If you were to ask these individuals, would they agree with your self-assessment?

REFLECT HERE...

This book may have stirred up the need for you to take action to make things right with people who you have wronged. Conviction can be a great tool to move you to correct your wrongs. This book may have caused you to recognize the need to take the steps to humble yourself. It may have led you to your knees to acknowledge the need to ask forgiveness. It may have led you to do one of the following stop statements. Regardless of how this book has "hit" you, I encourage you not just to read it and move on but to continue to take the time to self-reflect, self-assess, and take steps to make the necessary choices to readjust, change, and improve. Before moving on to the concluding chapter, reflect on the "stop" statements below and go beyond ascent. If you have exhibited any of the characteristics of the bad leadership characters from Chapter 5 (The Vile Witch, The Suck Up Lapdog, The "Oh No!" I Am in Over My Head, The Shady Sleaze, or The Pontius Pilate Sideliner), DO something about it, as you work through these "stop" statements.

- Stop mistreating people with your words. Be nice. Build others up. Share in their burdens. Realize that people are going through a lot in their personal lives and be gracious, giving others the benefit of the doubt.

- Stop saying and doing the same things repeatedly, expecting different results (remember Einstein once said this expectation was the definition of insanity).

- Stop overworking and underpaying your employees, and if you are in a religious company or organization, stop using God's word, the work to be done, and God's will as an excuse to mistreat people.

- Stop using your position of authority to elevate yourself, and in doing so, lose your reputation and testimony, and if you are a Christ-following, thus marring and ruining the character of Christ.

REFLECT HERE ON CHAPTER THOUGHTS, REACTIONS, RESPONSES, ACTION ITEMS...

CHAPTER NINE

FINAL THOUGHTS, REFLECTIONS, AND QUESTIONS TO PONDER

Leadership should leave a positive impression marked by a positively-remembered, impactful legacy. When looking back and reflecting on the places you have worked and the bosses you have had, you should be better due to the time you spent in a company or organization. Furthermore, if you have worked in a Christian environment with a Christian leader, the positive impact on you should be even higher. Stated that you should be better because of the leadership for whom you worked. The time and experience should have been worth it from a professional perspective and on your mental, physical, and spiritual health.

Throughout this book, we have consistently wrestled with the sad, opposite reality that many have faced with leadership. Companies and organizations are filled with bad leadership characters, even in Christian environments. So, in this concluding chapter, let us consider the following. What do we do when we encounter poor, ineffective leadership? How do we react to The Vile Witch, The Suck Up Lapdog, The "Oh No!" I Am in Over My Head, The Shady Sleaze, and The Pontius Pilate Sideliner? It is inevitable that we have faced these types of leaders in the past or will encounter them in the future.

WHAT TO DO, WHAT TO DO

When posed with the following prompt, here were some insightful, valuable thoughts from the many individuals who contributed to this book.

When working under poor, ineffective leadership, I should...

- Stay positive!
- Model servant leadership in all that I do.
- Step up to the plate and help where I can without being taken advantage of.
- Being an encouragement to others.
- If it is safe, be brave, humble, and vulnerable to share feedback with the leader. Everyone wants to do their job to the best of their ability. Not sharing feedback in a kind and humble way does not push leadership to grow and change. If leadership is not open to input or promotes an unsafe environment, it might be time to look for employment elsewhere.
- Talk to the leader in a kind but factual manner, noting what might be improved.
- Give positive feedback. If leadership is not open to feedback, it creates a hostile work environment. As an employee, you have just a few choices.
  - 1, take it higher up the chain of command.
  - 2, seek employment elsewhere.

- Neither is an easy task. One has to weigh their self-worth and make the right decision.
- Lead by example, encourage others who may be discouraged, and do my best to open conversation with the leader in hopes of seeing growth. Sometimes, despite your best efforts, you need to step away.
- Make suggestions that you think will improve operations
- Find others with similar values, form a pod, and work together to lead ourselves toward fulfilling & effective goals collectively.
- Find another place to work. People do not work for companies; they work for their leaders/management.
- Pray first.. for the boss and yourself.
- Be the best employee you can be and earn their respect.
- After that, the choices are so personal...can you afford to switch jobs?
- Then, is it possible to talk to your boss's boss? Or the human resources department on how to the situation? Can you bear to lose your job should all this backfire?
- If the conflict is just with you, it is an entirely different scenario from having all the employees frustrated with that boss. The course of action changes radically.
- Make my thoughts and ideas known that can assist the team/company. If they move in a different direction from what you obtained from their planned mission statement and where you imagined your career going, leave. It is not worth the unneeded stress. Your family is 100x important than playing in the worthless rat race.

- The order is always God, spouse, children, family, job. There are no other options. It is the only plan that works. People can be successful, but that does not equate to happiness/fulfillment. You MUST put God first, no exceptions.
- Set boundaries to ensure that I am not overwhelmed by the extra tasks and roles that stem from that.
- Do these things:
  - First, update your resume...
  - Second, finish well in the position and time you have committed to...
  - Third, if you have the conviction, do the hard thing and go to the "leadership" and state your thoughts through assessment of the situation before letting them know you will be leaving...
  - In so doing, you will feel much better taking that route.
- If they profess to be a Christian, address these issues according to Scripture.
- Speak up carefully, knowing you can do your job, but speaking up and walking away is the healthiest thing if it is that bad.

THE IMPORTANCE OF PRAYER

In the 1930s and 1940s, a prayer created by theologian Reinhold Niebuhr became popular throughout his sermons and church groups. Eventually, it was posted in a newspaper, and from there, a member of Alcoholics Anonymous picked it up, and now, the prayer is prevalent in many recovery groups and circles. Though there are various versions of

Niebuhr's now infamous prayer, his original prayer was overtly Biblical. It was intentionally based on the principles of Scripture related to suffering, struggle, and things in our lives that are often outside our control (Ford, 2018). Here is the full text of Niebuhr's original prayer (Quinn, 2023):

> God grant me the serenity
> To accept the things, I cannot change;
> Courage to change the things I can;
> And wisdom to know the difference.
> Living one day at a time;
> Enjoying one moment at a time;
> Accepting hardships as the pathway to peace;
> Taking, as He did, this sinful world
> As it is, not as I would have it;
> Trusting that He will make things right
> If I surrender to His Will;
> So that I may be reasonably happy in this life
> And supremely happy with Him
> Forever and ever in the next.
> Amen.

Serenity. It is a beautiful word with synonyms like calm, peaceful, tranquility, quiet. When dealing with difficult situations and people in our lives, serenity is not only a goal but can also be a blessing. Often, in these quiet, calm, serene moments, we can seek to make meaning and process life's intricate, challenging complexities. David said it this way in Psalm 46:10a. "Be still, and know that I am God." Niebuhr's prayer also illustrates the need to give up, trust, surrender, and let go. If you have suffered from a bad, ineffective leader, submit to God's will and plan, and accept the moments and seasons of hardship as an opportunity for growth.

In Scripture, many passages are related to suffering, with 53 instances of the words "suffer" and "suffering" (Bible Study Tools, 2024; ESV, 2001). Out of all of these instances, James gets straight to the point as he tells his readers in James 5:13a, "Is anyone among you suffering? Let him pray." In the same section in 5:16b, he says, "The prayer of a righteous person has great power as it is working." There are slight variances in how this verse appears in other translations (Bible Study Tools, 2024). Take note of the following:

- The prayer of a righteous person is powerful and effective. (NIV)
- The effectual fervent prayer of a righteous man availeth much. (KJV)
- A prayer of a righteous person, when it is brought about, can accomplish much. (NASB)
- The heartfelt and persistent prayer of a righteous man (believer) can accomplish much [when put into action and made effective by God—it is dynamic and can have tremendous power]. (Amplified)

Do you have a difficult boss? Pray. Do you feel the need to grumble, moan, and complain about your boss? Pray. Do you feel the need to slander and gossip about your boss? Pray. Do you feel mistreated and undervalued by your boss? Pray. Do you think you are overworked and underpaid? Pray. Do you feel your boss has favorites, and you are not one of them? Pray. Do you feel the urge to lash out at your boss? Pray. Do you feel the need to speak up for yourself? Pray. Do you see that your boss is making a colleague's life miserable? Pray. Are you working for The Vile Witch? Pray. Are you working for The Suck Up Lapdog? Pray. Are you working for The "Oh No!" I Am in Over My Head? Pray. Are you working for The

Shady Sleaze? Pray. Are you working for The Pontius Pilate Sideliner? Pray.

You get the point. Working for bad, ineffective leaders can allow all kinds of evil things to well up in our souls. Pray "that by doing good you should put to silence the ignorance of foolish people." (1 Peter 2:15b). Pray, and as necessary, keep praying without ceasing (1 Thessalonians 5:17). Sometimes, in the situational statements mentioned above, the right thing to do, or the right course of action, is nothing else and nothing more than choosing to pray. For what should you pray? This answer depends on your situation, but from Scriptural examples, you should pray for the heart and mindset of your brutal leader and that you have the right spirit, attitude, and behavior. Ask God for wisdom. Ask God for guidance. Ask God if you should speak up and advocate for yourself or others. Ask God for the strength to stand. And finally, as Paul wrote in 1 Corinthians 15:58, "Be steadfast, immovable, always abounding in the work of the Lord, knowing that in the Lord your labor is not in vain."

ENCOURAGEMENT FROM KING DAVID

In addition to the thoughts above related to prayer, I also trust that you, dear reader, find encouragement and solace in the words of David from 2 Samuel 22. It is a beautiful, raw, honest response from David to the Lord as he reflected on the deliverance provided by his enemies, especially from that of Saul, who was not a positive leader over David.

> [1] And David spoke to the Lord the words of this song on the day when the Lord delivered him from the hand of all his enemies, and from the hand of Saul. [2] He said,

"The Lord is my rock and my fortress and my deliverer, ³ my God, my rock, in whom I take refuge, my shield, and the horn of my salvation, my stronghold and my refuge, my savior; you save me from violence. ⁴ I call upon the Lord, who is worthy to be praised, and I am saved from my enemies.

⁵ "For the waves of death encompassed me, the torrents of destruction assailed me; ⁶ the cords of Sheol entangled me; the snares of death confronted me.

⁷ "In my distress, I called upon the Lord; to my God, I called. From his temple, he heard my voice, and my cry came to his ears.

⁸ "Then the earth reeled and rocked; the foundations of the heavens trembled and quaked because he was angry. ⁹ Smoke went up from his nostrils, and devouring fire from his mouth; glowing coals flamed forth from him. ¹⁰ He bowed the heavens and came down; thick darkness was under his feet. ¹¹ He rode on a cherub and flew; he was seen on the wings of the wind. ¹² He made darkness around him his canopy, thick clouds, a gathering of water. ¹³ Out of the brightness before him coals of fire flamed forth. ¹⁴ The Lord thundered from heaven, and the Most High uttered his voice. ¹⁵ And he sent out arrows and scattered them; lightning, and routed them. ¹⁶ Then the channels of the sea were seen; the foundations of the world were laid bare, at the rebuke of the Lord, at the blast of the breath of his nostrils.

¹⁷ "He sent from on high, he took me; he drew me out of many waters. ¹⁸ He rescued me from my strong enemy, from those who hated me, for they were too mighty for me. ¹⁹ They confronted me in the day of my calamity, but the Lord was my support. ²⁰ He brought

me out into a broad place; he rescued me because he delighted in me.

²¹ "The Lord dealt with me according to my righteousness; according to the cleanness of my hands, he rewarded me. ²² For I have kept the ways of the Lord and have not wickedly departed from my God. ²³ For all his rules were before me, and from his statutes, I did not turn aside. ²⁴ I was blameless before him, and I kept myself from guilt. ²⁵ And the Lord has rewarded me according to my righteousness, according to my cleanness in his sight.

²⁶ "With the merciful you show yourself merciful; with the blameless man you show yourself blameless; ²⁷ with the purified you deal purely, and with the crooked you make yourself seem tortuous. ²⁸ You save a humble people, but your eyes are on the haughty to bring them down. ²⁹ For you are my lamp, O Lord, and my God lightens my darkness. ³⁰ For by you I can run against a troop, and by my God, I can leap over a wall. ³¹ This God—his way is perfect; the word of the Lord proves true; he is a shield for all those who take refuge in him.

³² "For who is God, but the Lord? And who is a rock, except our God? ³³ This God is my strong refuge and has made my way blameless. ³⁴ He made my feet like the feet of a deer and set me secure on the heights. ³⁵ He trains my hands for war so that my arms can bend a bow of bronze. ³⁶ You have given me the shield of your salvation, and your gentleness made me great. ³⁷ You gave a wide place for my steps under me, and my feet[f] did not slip; ³⁸ I pursued my enemies and destroyed them, and did not turn back until they were consumed. ³⁹ I consumed them; I thrust them through

so that they did not rise; they fell under my feet. [40] For you equipped me with strength for the battle; you made those who rise against me sink under me. [41] You made my enemies turn their backs to me, those who hated me, and I destroyed them. [42] They looked, but there was none to save; they cried to the Lord, but he did not answer them. [43] I beat them fine as the dust of the earth; I crushed them and stamped them down like the mire of the streets.

[44] "You delivered me from strife with my people; you kept me as the head of the nations; people whom I had not known served me. [45] Foreigners came cringing to me; as soon as they heard of me, they obeyed me. [46] Foreigners lost heart and came trembling out of their fortresses.

[47] "The Lord lives, and blessed be my rock, and exalted be my God, the rock of my salvation, [48] the God who gave me vengeance and brought down peoples under me,

[49] who brought me out from my enemies; you exalted me above those who rose against me; you delivered me from men of violence.

[50] "For this I will praise you, O Lord, among the nations, and sing praises to your name. [51] Great salvation he brings to his king, and shows steadfast love to his anointed, to David and his offspring forever."

FINAL THOUGHTS AND A BLESSING

May God richly bless you and use this book in your life, specifically in your leadership development. May he give you the strength to stand firm and not falter when you encounter difficult people in leadership. May he give you the tools and resources to navigate challenging times and process difficulties from your past. May He provide you with the healing and relief of the burden of those who have wronged you. May He give you the strength to have the mind of Christ and positively impact those around you.

I leave you with a final blessing from a prayer of Moses, which is found in Psalms 90.

> [14] Satisfy us [God] in the morning with your steadfast love, that we may rejoice and be glad all our days. [15] Make us glad for as many days as you have afflicted us and for as many years as we have seen evil. [16] Let your work be shown to your servants and your glorious power to their children. [17] Let the favor of the Lord our God be upon us and establish the work of our hands upon us; yes, establish the work of our hands!

REFLECT HERE ON CHAPTER THOUGHTS,
REACTIONS, RESPONSES, ACTION ITEMS...

REFERENCES

Air Force Handbook 36-2618, Enlisted Force Structure, 16 May 2022.

Almes, B. (2019). *New DDI research: 57 percent of employees quit because of their boss.* Cision PR Newswire. https://www.prnewswire.com/news-releases/new-ddi-research-57-percent-of-employees-quit-because-of-their-boss-300971506.html

Beeson, J. (2012, August 22). *Deconstructing executive presence. Managing yourself: Developing executive presence.* Harvard Business Review. https://hbr.org/2012/08/de-constructing-executive-pres?autocomplete=true

Bible Study Tools (2024). Salem Web Network. https://www.biblestudytools.com/

Brown, M. E., Trevino, L. K., & Harrison, D. A. (2005). Ethical leadership: A social learning perspective for construct development and testing. *Organizational Behavior and Human Decision Processes, 97*(2), 117-134. https://doi.org/10.1016/j.obhdp.2005.03.002

Brzezinski, M. (2018, May 30). *With #MeToo, we need a serious talk about workplace ethics.* NBC News.

Retrieved October 25, 2019, from https://www.nbcnews.com/know-your-value/feature/metoo-we-need-serious-conversation-about-workplace-ethics-ncna830101.

Champagne, K. (2023). *Using leader-member exchange theory as a predictor of master sergeants' positive work outcomes.* [Doctoral Dissertation, Charleston Southern University]. ProQuest Dissertations and Theses Global.

Chapman, B. (2018). Situational leadership: A key leadership skill. *Leadership Excellence, 35*(9), 16. Retrieved from http://mendel.csuniv.edu/login?url=http?search.ebscohost.com/login.aspx?direct=true&db=5h&AN=135231031&site=eds-live&scope=site

Churchill, W. (1931). *Winston Churchill quotes.* Brainy Quotes. https://www.brainyquote.com/quotes/winston_churchill_130619#:~:text=Courage%20is%20the%20most%20important,but%20nothing%20consistently%20without%20courage.&text=Your%20time%20is%20limited%2C%20so,it%20living%20someone%20else's%20life.

Coleman, H., J. (2010, February 26). *Empowering yourself: The organizational game revealed.* AuthorHouse.

Colvin, J. (2021). *Everything rises and falls on leadership.* Pathways to Growth. https://www.pathwaystogrowth.us/everything-rises-and-falls-on-leadership#:~:text=According%20to%20John%20Maxwell%2C%20author,to%20invest%20in%20developing%20yourself

Creech, C. (2021). *EDUC701 Leadership Theory – Final Paper.* Unpublished document, Charleston Southern University.

Crenshaw, K. W. (1989). Demarginalizing the intersection of race and sex: A Black feminist critique of antidiscrimination doctrine, feminist theory, and antiracist politics. *University of Chicago Legal Forum, 1*(8)139–167. https://scholarship.law.columbia.edu

Currie, J. P., & Ryan, M. (2014). Complementing traditional leadership: The value of followership. *Reference and User Services Quarterly, 54*(2), 15–18. https://journals.ala.org/index.php/rusq/article/viewFile/2764/2752

DeWeil, J. (2024). *What the Bible says about leadership.* Newspring Church. https://newspring.cc/articles/what-the-bible-says-about-leadership

Doyle, A. (2017). Adaptive challenges require adaptive leaders. *Performance Improvement, 56*(9), 18. Retrieved from http://search.ebscohost.com.mendel.csuniv.edu/login.aspx?direct=true&db=edb&AN=125743426&site=eds-live&scope=site

Dudley, D. (2010). *Everyday leadership.* Retrieved November 1, 2019, from https://www.ted.com/talks/drew_dudley_everyday_leadership?language=en.

Elwell, W. A. (1997). Entry for 'Servant, Service.' *Evangelical Dictionary of Theology.* Baker Books. https://www.biblestudytools.com/dictionaries/bakers-evangelical-dictionary/servant-service.html

English Standard Version Bible. (2001). ESV Online. https://esv.literalword.com/

Evans, T. (2012). *The life of a kingdom man*. Sermons.Love. https://sermons.love/tony-evans/541-tony-evans-the-life-of-a-kingdom-man.html

Ehrlich, J. (December 6, 2011). *Developing executive presence*. Harvard Business Review. https://hbr.org/2011/12/developing-the-presence-of-an

Ford, H. B. (2018). *The serenity prayer and twelve-step recovery: Finding the balance between acceptance and change*. The Hazelden Betty Ford Foundation. https://www.hazeldenbettyford.org/articles/the-serenity-prayer#:~:text=There%20it%20was%20credited%20to,and%20other%20Twelve%20Step%20programs

Fries, K. (2018). *8 essential qualities that define great leadership*. https://www.forbes.com/sites/kimberlyfries/2018/02/08/8-essential-qualities-that-define-great-leadership/?sh=3e9782cb3b63

Gobble, M. M. (2017). The value of followership. *Research-Technology Management, 60*(4), 59- 63. https://doi.org/10.1080/08956308.2017.1325695

Greenleaf, R.K. (1977). *Servant leadership: A journey into the nature of legitimate power and greatness*. Paulist Press.

Hasan, S. (2024). *Top 15 leadership qualities that make good leaders*. TaskQue. https://blog.taskque.com/characteristics-good-leaders/

Heimann, N. (2020). Executive presence: Integrating the seven dimensions of leadership intelligence. *Leader to Leader, 2020*(96), 58-64.

Hemerling, J. (May, 2016). *5 Ways to lead in an era of constant change* [TED Talk]. Retrieved from https://www.ted.com/talks/jim_hemerling_5_ways_to_lead_in_an_era_of_constant_change

Heppner, S. and Wang, T. (2015, April 1). *What are the measurable qualities that define executive presence and how can we use it to tangibly assess leaders?* Cornell University Library Digital Collections. https://hdl.handle.net/1813/74513.

Heyler, S.G. & Martin, J.A. (2018). Servant leadership theory: Opportunities for additional theoretical integration. *Journal of Managerial Issues, 30*, 230-240

Hoover, J. (2011). *How to work for an idiot: Revised & expanded with more idiots, more insanity, and more incompetency: Survive and thrive without killing your boss.* Weiser.

Hyatt Fennell (2023). *Top traits of a horrible leader.* https://hyattfennell.com/top-traits-of-a-horrible-leader/

Kruse, K. (2013). *What is leadership?* Forbes Online. https://www.forbes.com/sites/kevinkruse/2013/04/09/what-is-leadership/?sh=51f02b7e5b90

Leading Effectively Staff (2023). *The 10 characteristics of an effective leader.* Center for Creative Leadership. https://www.ccl.org/articles/leading-effectively-articles/characteristics-good-leader/#:~:text=The%20 10%20Characteristics%20of%20a,respect%2C%20 empathy%2C%20and%20gratitude.

Linkin Park (2003). *Numb.* Meteroa. https://www.azlyrics.com/lyrics/linkinpark/numb.html

MacGuire, G. (2000). *Wicked: The life and times of the wicked witch of the West.* William Morrow.

Matchbox Twenty (1997). *Push.* Yourself or Someone Like You. https://www.lyrics.com/lyric/1089978/Matchbox+ Twenty/Push

Maxwell, J. (2019). *How to lead when your boss won't (or can't).* Harper Collins Leadership.

Maxwell, J. (2020). *Review of the 21 indispensable qualities of a leader: Becoming the person others will want to follow.* LeadershipNow. https://www.leadershipnow.com/ leadershop/7440-5.html

May, S. (2022). *10 quotes on leadership that will get you thinking.* Niagara Institute. https://www.niagarainstitute.com/blog/bad-leadership-quotes

McCallum, J. S. (2013). Followership: The other side of leadership. *Ivey Business Journal, 1*(1). https://iveybusiness journal.com/publication/followership-the-other-side-of-leadership/

McKinsey, De Smet, A., Dewar, C., Keller, S., Malhotra, V., & Srinivasan, R. (2021). *What is leadership?* https://www.mckinsey.com/featured-insights/mckinsey-explainers/what-is-leadership

Michael (2024a). *What is servant leadership? Characteristics, principles, and examples.* Leadership Geeks. https://www.leadershipgeeks.com/servant-leadership/

Michael (2024b). *Top 50 quotes about servant leadership.* Leadership Geeks. https://www.leadershipgeeks.com/servant-leadership-quotes/

N. A. (2018). *Rehoboam's failure to tell good advice from bad (2 Chronicles 10:1-19).* Theology of Work Project. https://www.theologyofwork.org/old-testament/samuel-kings-chronicles-and-work/from-failed-monarchies-to-exile-1-kings-11-2-kings-25-2-chronicles-10-36/rehoboams-failure-to-tell-good-advice-from-bad-2-chronicles-101-19/

N.A. (2023). *Decoding the 4 C's of leadership.* 31West. https://www.31west.net/blog/decoding-4-cs-leadership/#:~:text=Every%20leader%20makes%20mistakes.,Candor%2C%20Connect%2C%20and%20Character.

Northouse, P. G. (2019). *Leadership: Theory and practice* (8th ed.). Sage.

Northouse, P. G. (2021). *Leadership: Theory and practice* (9th ed). Sage.

Northouse, P.G. & Lee, M. (2019). *Leadership case studies in education.* Sage.

Owens, B. P., Yam, K. C., Bednar, J. S., Mao, J., & Hart, D. W. (2019). The impact of leader moral humility on follower moral self-efficacy and behavior. *Journal of Applied Psychology, 1*(146). Retrieved from http://search.ebscohost.com.mendel.csuniv.edu/login.aspx?direct=true&db=edsbl&AN=RN618740041&site=eds-live&scope=site

Prentice, W.C.H. (2004). *Understanding leadership.* Harvard Business Review Online. https://hbr.org/2004/01/understanding-leadership

Price, H. (2019). *6 examples of bad leadership.* https://blog.jostle.me/blog/6-examples-of-bad- leadership#:~:text=Lack%20of%20transparency&text=If%20leaders%20are%20withholding%20information,be%20as%20transparent%20as%20possible.

Quinn, D. (2023). *Serenity prayer: Finding help through hardship.* Sandstone Care. https://www.sandstonecare.com/blog/serenity-prayer/#:~:text=%E2%80%9CGod%20grant%20me%20the%20serenity,wisdom%20to%20know%20the%20difference.%E2%80%9D

Riggio, R. E. (2020). Why followership? *New Directions for Student leadership, 2020*(167), 15-22. https://doi.org/10.1002/yd.20395

Ritenbaugh, J. W. (2024). *What the Bible says about leaders are followers.* Bible Tools. https://www.bibletools.

org/index.cfm/fuseaction/Topical.show/RTD/cgg/ ID/20862/Leaders-are-Followers.htm

Robbins, T. (2024). *Elevate your impact: 10 leadership qualities of remarkable leaders.* Tony Robbins Guide. https://www. tonyrobbins.com/career-business/6-basic-leadership- qualities/

Rost, J. C. (1991). *Leadership for the twenty-first century.* Praeger.

Rothwell, W. J. (2010). *Effective succession planning: ensuring leadership continuity and building talent from within.* Amacom.

Saeed, S., & Ali, R. (2019). Relationship between authentic leadership and classroom management in public and private sector universities. *Journal of Education and Educational Development,* 6(1), 171–187. Retrieved from http://search.ebscohost.com.mendel.csuniv.edu/ login.aspx?direct=true&db=eric&AN=EJ1216786&site =eds-live&scope=site

Sage. (2023). *Description of leadership: Theory and practice by Peter G. Northouse.* https://us.sagepub.com/en-us/ nam/leadership/book270138#description

Scott, A. (2022). *EDUC701 Leadership Theory – Final Paper.* Unpublished document, Charleston Southern University.

Stasek, J. (2022). *6 qualities of a servant leader.* Wycliffe Bible Translators. https://www.wycliffe.org/blog/featured/6- qualities-of-a-servant-leader

Stewart, K. (2022). *Executive presence: Female leadership equity impediments.* [Doctoral Dissertation, Charleston Southern University]. ProQuest Dissertations and Theses Global.

Thomas, T., & Berg, P. (2020). The Army paradox: Leader and follower education. *New Directions for Student Leadership, 2020*(167), 111-122. https://doi.org/10.1002/yd.20403

Villanova University (2015). *The great man theory of leadership explained.* https://www.villanovau.com/articles/leadership/great-man-theory/

Walls, E. (2019). The value of situational leadership. *Community Practitioner, 92*(2), 31-33. Retrieved from http://mendel.csuniv.edu/login?url=http?search.ebscohost.com/login.aspx?direct=true&db=ccm&AN=135425015&site=eds-live&scope=site

Wicker-Miurin, F. (September, 2009) *Learning from leadership's missing manual.* Retrieved from https://www.ted.com/talks/fields_wicker_miurin_learning_from_leadership_s_missing_manual

Printed in the United States
by Baker & Taylor Publisher Services